TWAYNE'S WORLD AUTHORS SERIES

A Survey of the World's Literature

SPAIN

Gerald E. Wade and Janet W. Díaz
EDITORS

Juan Huarte de San Juan

TWAS 619

JUAN HUARTE DE SAN JUAN

By MALCOLM K. READ

The University College of Wales

TWAYNE PUBLISHERS
A DIVISION OF G. K. HALL & CO., BOSTON

Library of Congress Cataloging in Publication Data

Read, Malcolm Kevin, 1945–
Juan Huarte de San Juan.

(Twayne's world authors series ; TWAS 619 : Spain)
Bibliography: p. 127–31
Includes index.
1. Huarte de San Juan, Juan, 16th cent. Examen de ingenios.
2. Psychology—Early works to 1850.
BF115.H83R4   150'.92'4   80–22849
ISBN 0–8057–6461–5

Contents

About the Author

Preface

Acknowledgments

Chronology

1. The Elusive Author   13

2. The *Examen de ingenios*   25

3. The Flight from Doubt   35

4. The Sources   47

5. The Nature and Identity of Man   60

6. Reason versus Faith   72

7. Pedagogical Theory and Practice   85

8. Toward a Brave New World   99

9. The Influence of the *Examen*   106

10. Conclusion   125

Notes and References   129

Selected Bibliography   139

Index   145

About the Author

Malcolm Kevin Read was born in Derby, England, in 1945. He first studied in Bristol University, where he won a postgraduate scholarship for research on Spanish Golden Age linguistics. Since 1968 he has been Lecturer in Spanish in the Department of Romance Studies in the University College of Wales, Aberystwyth. In 1978–79 he was visiting Lecturer in Spanish in the Department of Romance Languages in Auckland University, New Zealand. He was awarded the degree of M. Litt. (Bristol) in 1972 and a Ph.D. (Wales) in 1978. He is the author of a variety of articles on Spanish linguistics and literature in many English, European, and American journals.

Preface

Juan Huarte de San Juan, author of a single, highly influential treatise on pedagogical psychology, the *Examen de ingenios para las ciencias* (1575), enjoyed in his own day an international reputation of truly imposing proportions. His work was translated into all the major European languages, including Latin, and ran into numerous editions. Its principal ideas became familiar to many leading scholars and philosophers, including, it has been claimed, Bacon, Descartes, Pascal, and Montesquieu. The extent of Huarte's fame may surprise the majority of students of Spanish, accustomed as they are to regard writers of imaginative literature as the leading lights of the Golden Age. Huarte is, in fact, one of a number of diverse Renaissance scholars and scientists who, though widely read in their own times, are now little known, except to specialists.[1] The reasons for the neglect in Huarte's case seem clear enough. His psychological teaching is based on classical sciences which have now been surpassed virtually in their entirety. In common with the leading scientists and compilers of knowledge of his day, such as Pedro Mexía and Cristóbal Suárez de Figueroa, Huarte has, in short, become the victim of the very progress in ideas which he himself so eloquently extolled. Similarly, he has become dated merely in the sense that some of his major preoccupations have ceased to be important, a fate he shares with such scholars as Vives and Erasmus. We are, for example, no longer vitally concerned with the question of the unique excellence of Latin, or the role of the vernacular (as opposed to Latin) in modern education.

However, there are reasons to lament the relative neglect into which Huarte's work has fallen. His contributions to the debate on some of the eternal, fundamental questions of human identity, such as that of the relationship between mind and body, were, by any standards, considerable, and deserve to figure more prominently in the history of ideas. Moreover, the rapid advance achieved in certain areas of science, such as physics and astronomy, has not been matched in other areas of investigation. Particularly in the field of psychology, traditional speculation remains in a very real sense unsurpassed, with the result that it can still be stimulating. It is indeed a fact that in recent years Huarte's emphasis on creativity as a distinctive attribute of man has attracted the opponents of behavioristic doctrines of human psychology.[2]

There is another reason for paying more attention to Huarte. The arts student who claims that such books as the *Examen* can be safely left to the historian of ideas or science seriously underestimates the extent to which these works contributed to the intellectual climate in which writers of imaginative literature were formed. Despite a marked drift toward specialization in the Renaissance, a drift which Huarte was so instrumental in fomenting, individuals were often at home in both the "arts" and "sciences" as we now understand them. There prevailed, in fact, a firm belief in the ultimate unity of culture, of which the *Examen* is also, in its own way, a most eloquent expression.[3] It comes as no surprise, therefore, to find that Huarte was indeed an important influence on imaginative literature. To begin with, the *Examen*, and works like it, provided the general background of physio-psychological categories with which creative writers would be familiar, and upon which they would draw, however indirectly. Such terms as *temperamento* ("temperament"), *destemplado* ("distempered"), *ingenio* ("wit"), etc., were part of the intellectual baggage of the educated man of the age, and it is important for the modern student to be aware of their meanings and implications for the Renaissance mind, these being rather different from those that the terms now have. Just as we would expect any serious critic of modern literature to be familiar with Freudian notions of the unconscious, which have been so pervasive in modern culture, so also we should expect the student of Renaissance literature to equip himself with a knowledge of the equally pervasive psychological doctrines in the period of his choice. Moreover, it seems that leading creative writers—Cervantes is commonly cited as an example—may have drawn directly on the *Examen* as regards certain dominant themes and ideas. And even if we find inconclusive the evidence for direct influence, it is clear that Huarte's fundamental preoccupations and perspectives closely resemble those of some of his eminent contemporaries in the field of imaginative literature, and that comparison between them can prove mutually revealing.

Though there have been a number of interesting articles in recent years dealing with the *Examen*, as yet no general survey of the work in English illustrates how Huarte's diverse interests and views fit into his total vision. Given the high quality of his thought, his continuing relevance to psychological investigation, and the extent of his influence, both on the literature of ideas and on imaginative literature, such a survey of his views would seem called for. The standard work in Spanish by Iriarte,[4] though still essential reading, is unsatisfactory and dated in certain respects. In attempting a general treatment of Huarte, I have naturally drawn extensively on contributions by other scholars, and this debt has, I trust, been fully acknowledged in the notes and bibliography. There are still gaps, of course, in our knowledge and understanding of Huarte, and I have tried to fill in some of these and indicate the nature of others; but at least part of my objective will have been achieved if I succeed in convincing the reader of the importance of this writer in European culture, and the need to deepen our understanding of his work.

My references throughout are to the edition of the *Examen* prepared by Esteban Torre (Madrid, 1976). The translations are my own.

MALCOLM K. READ

The University College of Wales

Acknowledgments

I am grateful to my colleagues in the Department of Romance Studies, at the University College of Wales, Aberystwyth, for their help and encouragement during the completion of this work. Needless to say, I absolve them from the faults that remain. I also wish to express my thanks to the University College of Wales, Aberystwyth, and to the British Academy for the provision of generous research grants; and to Mrs. Sheryl Bryan-Wells, who painstakingly typed the manuscript.

Chronology

c.1529   Juan Huarte born in San Juan de Pie de Puerto,
           Navarre (now Saint-Jean-Pied-de-Port in the De-
           partment of Basses-Pyrénées, France).
c.1530   Huarte's family emigrated, probably to Baeza in
           Andalusia.
c.1548–53 Studied at University of Baeza.
1553–59   Studied medicine at Alcalá.
1571–73   Held post of municipal doctor in Baeza.
1575   Published *Examen de ingenios*.
1588   Died. (or early 1589)
1594   Expurgated version of *Examen* printed.

CHAPTER 1

The Elusive Author

I *His Life*

DESPITE all the fame Huarte achieved in his own times and the highly personal tone of the *Examen de ingenios*, little is known for certain about his life.[1] The biographical details it is possible to glean from his work are few, and of debatable value. Even the form of his name is enigmatically vague. He signed his contracts and his will as "el doctor Juan de San Juan"; he is called "Doctor San Juan" by his contemporaries and also in a royal license to the Council of Baeza concerning his salary; whereas the title page of the *Examen* carried the name "Huarte," by which posterity has generally come to know him, though there appears to be no justification for "Juan Huarte Navarro," "Juan de Dios Huarte," and "Juan de Dios Huarte Navarro," as scholars have sometimes referred to him.[2] He was born in the small Pyrenean village of San Juan de Pie de Puerto, which was at the time of his birth ruled by Spain, but which is today part of France. The date of his birth is not known, and, since there are no parochial registers in San Juan prior to 1668, we have no way of discovering it. We may conjecture from what we know of his later career that it was about 1530. There is evidence to suggest that he had two sisters and one brother. The humbleness of his origins may explain his predilection, expressed in the *Examen*, for the simple, direct language of countrymen, as opposed to the elaborate diction of townsmen (pp. 182–83), and the vigor with which he proclaims that great men invariably originate in village stock (p. 276). Moreover, he took some positive pride in his birthplace, to judge by his persistent use of "de San Juan" when signing his name. It is believed that his family enjoyed a measure of local prestige, his grandfather being at one time the mayor of the village.

Huarte was destined to abandon the mountain fastness quite early in his life, when his parents emigrated to the south of Spain sometime between 1530 and 1540. One can only guess at the circumstances that attended this move. For instance, Huarte's father may have been a second son, obliged by the system of primogeniture prevailing in Navarre to seek his fortune elsewhere, like the *hidalgos* (i.e., lesser nobility) dependent upon their wit and resourcefulness whom his son was later to describe in his work. It is probable, however, that a key factor was the political turmoil accompanying the border dispute with France, in which San Juan de Pie de Puerto, by virtue of its proximity to the frontier, was much involved. Navarre had been incorporated into Castile in 1512 by Ferdinand the Catholic, but rebellious elements in the region, encouraged by France, continued to make their presence felt. San Juan was, in fact, besieged in 1516 by Jean d'Albret, who unsuccessfully attempted to recover his dominion from Spain. Unrest continued, despite the use of the Inquisition to drive out political dissidents, in addition to heretics (who had tended to seek refuge in the region). By 1530 Charles V had dismantled the fortifications of San Juan and ceased to collect tribute from its inhabitants.[3] Thus, from 1530 to 1660 (when it was incorporated into France), San Juan de Pie de Puerto was politically autonomous. This conferred a somewhat dubious status on its citizens, who were treated legally as foreigners in other parts of Navarre and were therefore subjected to considerable inconvenience and harassment. In these somewhat distressing circumstances, some families decided to abandon the region, emigrating not to other parts of Navarre and Aragon, where they were treated unfavorably, but to more distant parts of Spain. It seems very likely that Huarte belonged to such a family, and that Baeza, in Andalusia, became his new hometown.

The move must have occurred early in Huarte's life, for he himself refers to Spanish as his mother tongue ("my Spanish" [p. 166]), and recounts, presumably on the basis of personal experience, the ease with which a Basque child, in contrast to an adult, acquires the Romance vernacular on moving to Toledo (p. 165). However, Huarte was sensitive to the effects of being "deprived of the favor and protection of [one's] native land" (p. 75), a fact which may suggest a lingering sense of alienation in his new land, aggravated by a natural reticence and shyness.

It has often been suggested that Huarte studied and graduated at the University of Huesca,[4] though the relevant documentary evidence only indicates that a doctor San Juan *lectured* in Huesca from 1569 to 1570. This could have been the author of the *Examen*, but it is doubtful whether he was ever associated with this university either as a student or as a teacher.[5] Most scholars now accept that it was at Baeza that Huarte studied. This was at the time a rich and dynamic city, and its university, though provincial, was not undistinguished. In Baeza Huarte would receive the usual grounding in traditional Aristotelian physics and metaphysics, mathematics and languages. The fact that he seems to have graduated at the late age of twenty-two or twenty-three has led some scholars to suggest that he interrupted his studies with journeys to Europe, or a spell in the army in Milan or Naples, where, it is argued, he would have acquired his considerable knowledge, exhibited in the *Examen*, of both military strategy and the national characteristics of Europeans.[6]

After completing his studies in Baeza, Huarte went to follow a course in medicine in the University of Alcalá in 1553, a move which was doubtless to lead him to reflect in the *Examen* on the advantages of a student's being educated away from hometown and family environment (p. 75). Alcalá was at the time one of the foremost European centers of medical studies, boasting such famous lecturers as Cristóbal de Vega and Francisco Valles, though lecturers and students, to judge again by Huarte's own comments in the *Examen*, were of variable quality. Huarte reveals considerable anecdotal knowledge concerning Alcalá, particularly with respect to Antonio de Nebrija, one of its most famous early teachers, whose considerable reputation appears to have lingered on in Huarte's time (pp. 191–92). Huarte took his *bachillerato* in medicine in 1555 and, after a further series of courses, became a *licenciado* in 1559. He was granted the title of doctor in the same year.

Then follows another of those curious periods in Huarte's life when he disappears from all records, though it is known that it was during this period he married Doña Agueda de Velasco, also of Basque émigré stock. It is supposed that he practiced medicine, possibly teaching in the University of Huesca, which would explain the identity of the Doctor San Juan who lectured there in 1569–70. He certainly owned a house in Tarancón and had business interests in Corral de Almaguer and Villarejo de Salvanés.[7] He eventually moved to Linares, where he lived until his death, and where his daughter was baptized and his wife, whom he outlived, was buried. Though later to become important through the exploitation of its lead mines, Linares at this time was basically a satellite of Baeza. It was the civic authorities of Baeza, in fact, who in 1571 offered Huarte the post of official municipal doctor for a period of two years, following an outbreak of plague. In 1914 there was discovered in the town's municipal archives the license from Philip II (dated February, 1572) granting permission for Huarte to practice in Baeza. It contains the following: ". . . because all the old and experienced doctors of the aforementioned city [Baeza] had died and there remained only young doctors, inexperienced in their profession, you had tried, for the good and well-being of the inhabitants of the aforenamed city, and in order that they should be better cared for, to bring to the said city a suitable doctor, and thus you had brought Dr. Juan de San Juan, who was a suitable person for the said city and its citizens, and of whom you had heard that he was a man of great learning. . . ."[8] Details of Huarte's salary are given. The appointment was not renewed, and his will indicates the city of Baeza still owed him money at his death.

Huarte presumably lived off his private practice after his civic appointment was terminated, though he appears to have retained a house in Baeza. We know nothing of his professional activities, and evidence regarding his efficiency is conflicting. It has been suggested that he was good at his job, and in this way acquired the local reputation which led to his civic appointment.[9] There are other indications, however, that he was not a great success. He himself seems to imply that he was strong on the theoretical side and weak on the practical (p. 229 ff.), and, insofar as he considers the "mechanical" arts to be unworthy of attention (p. 278), he was probably proud of his bias. Even his interest in vivisection was perhaps a mere recollection from his student days or from his reading of Galen.

During these years Huarte was reflecting on those problems that most intrigued him scientifically, and planning and writing his life's work. It has been claimed, on the basis of internal evidence, that the *Examen* was already written in 1557, but this evidence is not compelling.[10] In any event it was certainly completed by 1574, and published the following year in Baeza. New editions followed quickly and the French and Italian translations were undertaken, but in 1583 the work was placed on the Index (the list of books forbidden to Roman Catholics) in Spain, having been previously banned in Portugal. Huarte, however, had not abandoned his investigations with the publication of the *Examen*, and he would probably have produced his own new edition even if the first had escaped the attention of the Inquisition and the task of revision not been forced upon him. Hence, the revised posthumous edition of 1594 contains many alterations and additions, some of them very substantial, not demanded by the holy body.

Huarte had seven children, three boys and four girls. Somewhat ironically, in view of the final chapter of the *Examen* on the niceties of genetic selection, they seem to have lacked their father's brilliance, though it was Huarte's son Luis who prepared and saw through the press the 1594 edition of his work. One of Huarte's daughters took the veil, and died in 1644 at the age of eighty as the Abbess of the Convent of Santa Catalina in Baeza. Though his wife and daughters always used the title of "doña," Huarte's will shows he was not a wealthy man. His relative poverty is confirmed by the lack of ostentation in his funeral rites, in an age when these were habitually elaborate. He died, probably in Baeza, in 1588 or early 1589, at about the age of sixty. He requested in his will, which contains an open confession of faith, that he be buried in Linares in the Church of Santa María, though no trace of his own or his wife's grave has been found. Thus, in death as in life, Huarte remains an elusive figure.

II *The Times*

The early decades of the sixteenth century in Spain witnessed a rich cultural flowering. More than one generation of Spanish intellectuals travelled to Italy to imbibe the new learning of the Renaissance at its source, and returned to their homeland with plans for reform. Antonio de Nebrija (1441–1522) was perhaps the most prominent of the early Spanish Humanists, studying for several years in the Spanish college of St. Clement's in Bologna. He initially chose the University of Salamanca to begin his crusade of enlightenment, but later moved to the University of Alcalá, at which Huarte was later to study and which had been founded in 1508 by Cardinal Ximénez de Cisneros. The new university soon began to rival Salamanca, thanks to the efforts of such scholars as Nebrija. It was noted for its breadth of syllabus and the intellectual freedom which it fostered, and Huarte's own intellectual vigor undoubtedly owes much to the stimulating environment he encountered there. In these early years Italy was not the only formative influence on Spanish Humanism, for Spain also looked very much to northern Europe. Erasmianism was fervently received and widely disseminated in some quarters. Erasmus himself was favorably considered by Charles V, who, though not a man of great intellect, was of liberal outlook, and encouraged and protected those similarly inclined.

By the time of Huarte's birth, however, black clouds had begun to gather on the horizon. In 1517 Luther nailed his ninety-five theses to the cathedral door at Wittenberg and the Catholic-Protestant breach soon gaped wide. Even in Spain there was a real threat to religious unity, despite the successful efforts of reformers such as Cardinal Ximénez to cleanse the Church of the grossest features of corruption. Inevitably, the Inquisition, which was entrusted with the care and maintenance of this unity, experienced a new lease of life. It is not clear whether there existed any real Protestant converts in Spain, for the Church tended to condemn as Lutheranism all departures from the narrowest orthodoxy. But Erasmians there were, and these, together with any other vaguely Protestant sects, were rooted out and ruthlessly persecuted and destroyed. Erasmus, it is true, had dissociated himself from Luther by 1525, but his reputation in Spain was already irreparably tarnished and his supporters found safety only in exile.[11]

Thus, Spain threw its weight behind the Counter-Reformation and began to assume all the features of a closed society. Creative writers had little to fear, provided they did not openly transgress the bounds of orthodoxy, and indeed Spain's literary renaissance was to continue for many years, reaching its peak toward the end of the century. But for intellectuals in general, and particularly for polemical writers professing such advanced and daring views as Huarte, committed to a wide-ranging, unflinching investigation into some of the profoundest issues concerning man, this was a frustrating, sometimes humiliating, and consistently dangerous age in which to live. Though there is no evidence to suggest academics were more systematically persecuted than other groups by the Inquisition, those upholding the spirit of free inquiry were bound to suffer particular oppression in a society that had surrendered its freedom in the interests of religious unity and orthodoxy. Predictably, some of Spain's most eminent scholars, including Fray Luis de León, Gaspar de Grajal, and Martín Martínez de Cantalapiedra, along with Francisco Sánchez "el Brocense," fell afoul of the Inquisition.[12]

Alcalá was notable for the number of Erasmians associated with its cloisters: Mateo Pascual, a former professor, was tried and sentenced by the Inquisition; Juan de Valdés, one of its most famous pupils, found it prudent to hasten into exile; Pedro de Lerma, the former chancellor of the University, was denounced, imprisoned in 1537, and died in exile in Paris; and over the next few decades more Alcalá scholars were persecuted for their suspect views.[13] Although in Huarte's student days in the 1550s something of the old enlightened, crusading spirit lingered on, the University, as the upholder of liberal studies, was well into decline.

The situation continued to worsen throughout Huarte's life. The first official engagement of the new king, Philip II, in 1559 was to preside over an *auto da fé* in Valladolid. In the same year the first Index of the Inquisition appeared, listing among others works by Erasmus and Fray Luis de Granada. By the time Huarte came to publish the *Examen* in 1575, the entrenched forces of conservatism were completely in control, and progressive scholars such as himself learned to tread with care, ever sensitive to the ominous presence of the Inquisition. Circumspectly he expressed his disapproval of the Lutheran heresy and was critical of Erasmus (pp. 180, 201), but the marks of the latter's influence are clearly apparent in the *Examen*;[14] and Huarte came to formulate a theory of biological determinism which was in essential respects a scientific counterpart of Luther's theology of predestination. Thus, it seems inevitable with hindsight that he should have become yet another victim of the holy tribunal and have been obliged to "toe the party line." Ironically, as in the case of Fray Luis de León and others, it was the University, in this case that of Baeza, that first alerted the Inquisition to the potential heretic.[15]

There is reason to believe Lutheran heresy was not the only cloud to darken Huarte's existence. The religious persecution and intolerance accorded to the Erasmians and Protestants in Spain had long been the lot of the Jewish community, which had been subjected to all kinds of abomination since the Middle Ages. In 1492 the Catholic monarchs gave the Jews a choice between exile and conversion. Of the great mass of "new Christians" or *conver-*

sos who remained in Spain, many continued to practice the old faith, and often suffered thereby at the hands of the Inquisition. Huarte's impassioned praise of the Jews suggested to one of his early critics, Jourdain Guibelet, that "one would easily suspect him of having had in his soul a trace of Judaism. . . ."[16] For Guibelet this was one more reason to denounce the Spaniard's work: ". . . I have found in this treatise called the *Examen* numerous evil drugs mixed with a little Judaism. . . ."[17] Modern critics, however, have generally failed to take up Guibelet's theory. One reason for this could be that they have been discouraged and repelled by the anti-Semitism that inextricably accompanied the Frenchman's claims (e.g., ". . . the Jews do not have more elevated minds, but are merely more skilful in deceit, than most other nations"[18]). Alternatively, it could be a species of anti-Semitism itself that has led scholars to ignore the possibility of Huarte's being of *converso* status. As Stephen Gilman notes, the Jewish origins of eminent Spaniards in the past are "first of all denied, . . . ; then, if the denial cannot stand up in the face of the evidence, they are ignored."[19]

The most outspoken leading critic of such duplicity has long been Américo Castro, who in several major works has developed the theory that the historical and cultural development of modern Spain can only be fully understood in the light of the racial conflict between Jew and Christian. Castro does not deal with Huarte and the *Examen* in any depth, and sometimes even fails to mention the physician in his lists of leading Spanish *conversos*, extensive and speculative though these are.[20] Nevertheless, there seems little doubt in Castro's mind that Huarte was indeed of Jewish extraction. He draws attention to the physician's interest in the history of the Jews, to his discussion of the effects on these people of persecution and social repression,[21] and to his "scientific explanation" (corresponding to a popularly held belief) as to why intellectual acumen may be seen as typically *converso*.[22] Castro also argues that Huarte's rejection of miraculous explanation in science and his direct appeal to the Bible and avoidance of popular, ecclesiastical Christianity "suggest that he was probably a New Christian."[23] Confessing the lack of documentary evidence, he yet feels able to speculate that Huarte's family may have been among those unable to leave Navarre following the expulsion of the Jews from Spain.[24]

The failure of scholars to follow up these leads has been unfortunate, for though nothing specific in the scanty biographical details of Huarte's life proves that he was a *converso*, there are indications of Judaic provenance in addition to those discussed by Castro. To begin with, the very dearth of information concerning Huarte's life and the sense of his almost willful anonymity could perhaps be explained by his *converso* status, rather than by a natural reticence. Whereas Luis Vives and Francisco Sánchez the Skeptic found security from racial prejudice in exile, and Fernando de Rojas in authorial anonymity, Huarte might have sought it in personal privacy and self-effacement. Given the severe religious intolerance of the age, his protestations of faith could have been nothing more than a wise precaution. Similarly, certified burial in sacred ground was essential for a *converso* anxious to dispel the suspicion that his very status generated;[25] and testaments, by establishing the orthodoxy of the deceased, ensured that his inheritance passed to his family rather than into the hands of the Inquisition.[26] Moreover, the fact that one of Huarte's children entered orders is not in itself a guarantee of the sincerity of his faith, for *converso* families, whether through true personal conviction or the hope of financial advancement, traditionally gave many sons and daughters to the Church.[27]

The medical profession was virtually monopolized by Jews in the Middle Ages, a fact which helps to explain the disdain in which it was popularly held, and, after 1492, when the Jews faced the choice of exile or conversion, *converso* doctors continued their work. Henry Kamen records how, at the end of the sixteenth century, a desperate Municipality of Logroño was forced to employ a certain Dr. Bélez, a *converso*, being unable to discover an Old Christian who was sufficiently qualified for the post. The appointment was confirmed in Madrid, but on the understanding that Dr. Bélez should not be granted official status, in the hope that an Old Christian would eventually be found.[28] Despite such opposition, however, *converso* doctors rose to eminent positions. Dr. Francisco Villalobos attended both Ferdinand the Catholic and Charles V, and Dr. Andrés de Laguna, also a famous naturalist and botanist, was physician to the Pope. Kamen sums up: "The outstanding services of the 'conversos' to medicine are amply illustrated by the number of doctors who appear in the records of the Inquisition during the sixteenth and seventeenth centuries."[29]

Huarte does not hesitate to praise the medical expertise of the

Jews at considerable length. He tells, for example, the story of
how Francis I of France sent a letter to Charles V of Spain re-
questing a Jewish doctor to cure a lingering complaint from
which he was suffering. Charles was naturally unable to find one
in his own kingdom, but sent instead a New Christian. When
Francis discovered from the doctor—Huarte records their conversation in detail in a rather novelistic manner—that he was not, in
fact, Jewish, he proceeded to dismiss him, "because I have
enough Christian doctors in my own court" (p. 238). The French
king was eventually cured, so the story goes, by a Jewish doctor
whom he discovered in Constantinople.

Huarte considers the question of Jewish expertise in medicine
within the context of a more general discussion of the influence of
climate and diet upon the intellect. He traces the history of the
Jews through their sojourn in Egypt, where the excessive heat
caused hypertrophy of their imaginative faculty (p. 241). This
development was stimulated during their ensuing exile in the
desert by the quality of the manna on which they fed (pp.
243–44), the air they breathed, and the water they drank (pp.
244–45). Insofar as he believed practical skill in medicine is
dependent upon the imagination, the author of the *Examen*
found Jewish excellence in this profession quite predictable and
unquestionable.

Huarte was obliged to modify his environmental theory in
order to explain the Jews' continuing virtuosity in medicine,
despite their having taken up residence in numerous other countries in the course of the centuries since Christ. Clearly, a change
in environment argued logically for a change in intellect. In order
to circumvent this problem, Huarte suggests that some accidental
qualities, when acquired, are short-lived, whereas others linger
on (p. 248). He adduces other subtle arguments relating to diet
and the qualities of manna, and concludes: "The fact is that they
[the descendents of the people of Israel] are as quick-witted and
intelligent now as they were a thousand years ago. It is true that
they began to lose their distinctive wit as soon as they ceased to
eat manna, and began to live off other foods, inhabit regions
other than Egypt, and intermarry with gentiles, who lack this
wit. But it cannot be denied that they still have not lost it
entirely" (pp. 251–52).

Certain other aspects of Huarte and his work assume fresh

significance when considered in the light of his possible *converso* status. Most notably there is that striking contrast between the calmness and tranquillity of his outward life and the inner turmoil of his mind. Castro has described how the *converso*, imprisoned socially within his caste, turned in upon himself and found consolation and release in the private pursuit of intellectual truth.[30] It is hard to read the *Examen*, particularly the prefatory material, without being struck by the introversion of the author and the self-consciousness with which he discusses his own intellectual development and the workings of man's mind. If Huarte fascinated some of the great creative writers of his day to the extent that seems possible, it was perhaps because, as a *converso*, he was striving in his own field to come to terms with the same identity crisis as they were.

Huarte's obsessive concern to exclude religious considerations from his scientific investigation reminds us that the *converso* was also typically skeptical and irreligious, committed above all to a rationalistic view of life.[31] Though not an atheist or agnostic in the modern sense of these terms, the *converso*, forced to abandon his own religion and unable to embrace sincerely that of his oppressors, sometimes surrendered to doubt and uncertainty. Concealment of views and ambiguity of expression became necessary and instinctive. Huarte certainly appears to be lacking in any religious sensibility, and does not hesitate to subject the character of Christ to psychological examination and to analyze the Bible in scientific terms. Inhabiting a private world in which God was intellectually and emotionally otiose and surrounded by a society in which passion rather than reason held sway, he, like many *conversos*, finally took refuge in Alcalá.

Castro suggests that it was politically ambitious Jews, and later *conversos*, who provided much of the enthusiasm behind movements toward social reform, an enthusiasm somewhat dampened by the oppressions of Inquisitorial Spain.[32] This seems a possible context in which to focus Huarte. Though at first glance a champion of progress, he was basically resigned and pessimistic, and held no hope that society could be reformed in the radical manner it really required. Whatever his actual status, he shared the *converso*'s resentment of the ignorance of his fellowmen. Particularly in the revised version of the *Examen*, he emerges as a man who feels misunderstood and oppressed by a barbarous, malicious world, resigned, like other rationalists of his day, to his inability to stem the rising tide of bigotry and intolerance.

Several minor facts might be mentioned in a consideration of Huarte's possible *converso* status. Firstly, Huarte, like many *conversos*, was intensely interested in magic, as a corollary to his rationalism. The practitioners of the black arts were traditionally of Jewish stock, and medical theory was steeped in superstition. In his attempt to rationalize magic and insanity and incorporate it into his psychological doctrine, Huarte captures perfectly the *converso* yearning to explain and control the supernatural. Secondly, it could also be suggested that Huarte's love of his homeland, with his interest in race and hereditary genetics, may reflect the *converso*'s habitual fascination with all that gave a sense of permanence and stability to his fundamentally precarious world. Thirdly, perhaps it was the insecurity of his marginal status in society that also led Huarte, like many *conversos*, to seek a basis for personal evaluation in such superficial criteria as honor, rank, dress. We are reminded that the *Examen* includes one of the most widely quoted sixteenth-century treatments of *hidalguía* (i.e., nobility). Lastly, it should be noted that *conversos*, in their quest for social acceptance, often claimed descendence from the Old Christians of the Basque country or Asturias and the northern mountains, who had begun the fight to win back Spain from the pagans. This might explain Huarte's constant concern to remind people that he hailed from San Juan.

In conclusion, the above considerations, while providing nothing more than circumstantial evidence, would seem to argue persuasively in favor of the view that Huarte was indeed one of the talented group of *converso* writers, which includes Fernando de Rojas, Luis Vives, Santa Teresa de Avila, Fray Luis de León, the Blessed Juan de Avila, and Sánchez the Skeptic, who made such important and original contributions to Spanish and European culture in the Renaissance.

CHAPTER 2

The Examen de ingenios

I *The Book*

HUARTE wrote only one work, the *Examen de ingenios para las ciencias*, into which he poured all that he had come to believe about the human condition, after years of careful thought and observation. The result was a panoramic view of scholarship and, ultimately, a total vision of the identity of man. It only remained for him in the revised edition to deepen insights achieved and perfect the details of what had already been said.

Despite the grandeur of the enterprise, the *Examen* had its genesis in very specific circumstances. Huarte tells us that he was puzzled as to why, when he and two fellow pupils entered upon the study of Latin together, only one excelled; whereas when they passed on to mathematics, one of the two who had been weak at Latin surpassed the other two; and the remaining student, weak in both Latin and mathematics, performed far better than the other two at astrology. The questions raised by these diverse aptitudes, trivial though they may have seemed to others, absorbed Huarte's thoughts—he confesses to having been "over-awed"—and he meditated upon them and explored their different facets with absorption. What kinds of wit (*ingenio*) are there to be found in men? What sciences are suited to what wits? How can each wit be recognized? Can we influence and control the wit of the unborn child? The more he thought about such problems the more profoundly intriguing the subject seemed, and he began to philosophize, giving full rein to his inventive spirit.

Yet Huarte was the least irresponsible of scholars, not given to idle flights of imagination, and, at the very start of his enterprise, he hesitated. The awesome complexity of the problems he proposed to deal with, and the very difficulties attending his attempts to penetrate the privacy of man's inner being, led him to reflect upon the nature of truth and the existence of criteria of verification. Thus, he first explored the possibility of the progressive discovery of truth, by a strict adhesion to rational principles and the close study of reality. Only then did he proceed to come to terms with those fundamental problems that most intrigued him, though doubts concerning the validity of his methodology, occasioned in part by the development of his ideas as he proceeded, continued to plague him and manifest themselves throughout his work.

He accepted as axiomatic that all souls are equal, but noted that, irrespective of the teaching received and the *art* and willpower applied to a particular intellectual task, some men are by *nature* more skilled than others. Huarte explained these facts in terms of men's "temperamental" imbalance. The common matter of the universe is built up of four elements—air, water, fire, and earth—which pass into the body in the food we eat and the air we breathe, to become the four humors which are the life-giving force of the body. The qualities associated with these humors are causally related, via the brain, to the faculties of the rational soul. Hence, an imbalance in them causes men to excel or to fail in different ways intellectually. Severe imbalance leads to pathological impairment and, in some cases, to insanity, a subject of abiding fascination for Huarte and one he explored in some detail.

Although he accepted that there exists a unique mixture in each individual, Huarte believed it possible to discern certain general categories of intelligence in men. He identified three major kinds of wit, both quantitatively and qualitatively. Quantitatively, some men are able to learn only passively, by response to stimuli; others exhibit much more ability, but are still basically parasitic upon their teachers; whereas others are capable of truly creative activity. Qualitatively, there also exist three categories, according to which of the three faculties of the mind may dominate an individual.

This framework provided a basis for Huarte's categorization of the sciences, and a plan for the rationalization of pedagogical selection in contemporary institutions of education. Ideally, Huarte claimed, educational authorities should ascertain the dominant faculty of the individual, so as to be able to direct him toward that discipline for which he is naturally best equipped. The same framework also enabled Huarte to treat such absorbing problems as the nature of the soul, the degree of its dependence on the body, and the implications of these matters as regards free will and predestination or determinism. Christianity encouraged a belief in the independence of the immortal soul from the corrupt body, which is discarded at death. It also considered the soul to be unequivocally the dynamic partner, directing and influencing the body. Huarte's empiricism, on the other hand, led him to take the body as his starting point, and to emphasize the importance of somatic factors. Hence, unlike the orthodox Christian thinker, Huarte was inclined, however inadvertently, to see man's behavior as governed by forces originating ultimately in the physical world. This was naturally crucial to the question of man's free will. In Huarte's scheme the scope of man's freedom of action is severely circumscribed. Huarte undoubtedly tried to moderate his determinism, but it is difficult to decide whether he did so through genuine conviction or mere circumspection.

The work concludes with a section on eugenics, where he discusses the practical measures to be taken to produce talented children, and boys as opposed to girls, along with such matters as child care and the matching of marital partners so as to aid conception. Huarte's discussion throughout, though couched in the accepted terms of classical chemistry, physiology, and psychology, was original and incisive, and his work was widely read, influencing not only creative writers, critics, and theorists of literature, but also philosophers, theologians, and grammarians in Spain and Europe.

II   *The Publication and Reception of the* Examen

The first printing of the *Examen* in Baeza in 1575 was paid for by the author. Though Baeza was not noted for its editorial activity, a fact which might have delayed any immediate impact,[1] the work was soon attracting attention. In 1578 the Pamplona edition appeared, followed by those of Valencia and Bilbao two years later, and by that of Huesca in 1581. By this time the French translation was available (1580), and the Italian translation soon followed (1582). This kind of success must have been flattering. One imagines that initially the title provoked some curiosity, and that people read the work to discover their own wit, rather in the way people today are given to reading popularizations of psychology, in order to gain some insight into their own natures. However, Huarte's vigorous statement of his views must soon have compelled more discriminating study. One can well imagine also that the work upset certain people from the beginning. Its personal, anecdotal nature probably led readers to think, correctly or incorrectly, that real living people were being alluded to directly in the pages of the *Examen*. They would be encouraged to think in this way by Huarte's habit of naming his patients in case studies in the interests of scientific exactitude, for he appears to have been notably lacking in the professional discretion of modern medical practitioners.

Other people were doubtless upset by the categories imposed on them in the *Examen*. The denunciation of the work, in fact, appears to have derived from Dr. Alonso Pretel, a professor of theology at Baeza University and commissary in that town to the Holy Inquisition. It has been suggested that he was offended by Huarte's categorization of his discipline (under memory, as opposed to understanding).[2] His denunciation was passed on to the Inquisition in Córdoba, and eventually to the central body in Madrid.[3] Moreover, Dr. Pretel and his fellow professors at Baeza must have been somewhat scandalized by the temerity of this provincial physician, who, within the portals of their very own institution, had dared to advocate a "new mode of philosophizing."

Finally, the more detailed examination of the text revealed that some of the author's views were highly controversial and, indeed, of questionable orthodoxy from the religious point of view. Not only isolated passages and comments but whole sections of the *Examen* seemed suspect. To take but one example, Huarte clearly stated that preachers, by virtue of their weakness in matters pertaining to the understanding, are ill qualified to reveal the true meaning of the Scriptures. This meaning, he believed, is accessible to any man "naturally" equipped to cope with the task of interpretation. Exactly what he meant by this he saw as his duty to explain in his work; but it should have been obvious that no amount of rational explanation would ever convince the Inquisitors. Indicative of this is the fact that a twenty-one-year-old student, Diego Alvarez, had in 1578 already directed against Huarte a critical analysis of his work entitled *Animadversión y enmienda de algunas cosas que se deben corregir en el libro que se intitula "Examen de ingenios."*

Thus, despite the favorable *censura* (i.e., license for publication) from the pen of the famous, learned, and highly orthodox Jesuit, Lorenzo de Villavicencio, and Huarte's tactful use (unstated but clearly implicit) of Philip II as a model of kingship in chapter XIV of the *Examen*, some or all of the above factors combined to provoke an official reaction. By 1581 the *Examen* had appeared on the Portuguese Index, and by 1583 on the Spanish Index, although editions continued to appear in the Low Countries and abroad. The following year, 1584, a list of required expurgations was given, some forty-four in all, of varying length, from odd words to the whole of chapter VII. The Spanish Index, unlike the Italian, could both expurgate works and ban them *in toto*. In some cases it was probably Huarte's manner of expression that was the main cause of offense. For example, noting the tendency of people to explain events in terms of the miraculous, Huarte writes that "philosophers of nature ridicule this manner of speaking," though he confesses that "it is pious and contains within it religion and truth . . ." (p. 80). Not surprisingly, the Inquisition demanded the deletion of the whole section in which these statements were made. Other sections were clearly seen to be radically objectionable, such as chapter VII, which dealt with the soul and the nature of its relationship with the body.

Huarte himself had no desire for martyrdom. He must have been aware of his vulnerability to attack from an institution that included among its victims figures far more eminent than he. He had anticipated in part the reaction his book was to produce, for he took care in his prefatory remarks to warn the reader of the novelty of his views and the likelihood that they would, initially at least, cause some offense; and he went so far as to warn those who believed that Truth was already discovered, or who were too intellectually limited to appreciate true learning, not to read his work. His curiosity and self-doubt were, however, alien to the officials of the Inquisition who had no doubt as to what Truth was, and certainly none as to what it was not. Thus, Huarte was obliged to work on a new edition, which was published posthumously in Baeza in 1594 under the supervision of his son.

In contrast to the first edition, whose impeccable presentation as regards its printed form suggests the guiding hand of the author himself, the new edition, censured, amended, and expanded, was carelessly prepared and is frequently confusing. A comparison between the two editions reveals the extent to which Huarte was obliged to change and qualify his views, and even make statements that he personally disagreed with. For example, the section criticizing those people who explain natural events in terms of the miraculous has been completely recast: "Among natural philosophers and the unlettered, the rational and causal explanation of a given effect is a subject of great controversy. Some people, when they see a man of great intellect and ability, point to God as the sole author and consider no other factor. And they are quite right in this . . ." (p. 383). Nevertheless, it is also obvious that, despite considerable superficial revision, Huarte "took every opportunity to make apparent his true, incorruptible position."[4] Hence, for example, the physician continues his revised discussion of causation by reiterating that "[w]hat natural philosophers cannot tolerate is that, when the reason and cause of a given effect is being sought, one should stop at the first [i.e., God], and fail to seek and take into account the influence of secondary causes . . ." (p. 384).

As has been noted, Huarte also took the opportunity in the second edition to carry out his own modifications and expansions. Some of these, particularly those dealing with the subject of creativity, are of notable interest and reveal Huarte's continuing and increasingly penetrating analysis of the problems he had initially posed; but others are undoubtedly leaden, and their excessive number of quotations and references to "authorities" suggests that Huarte had lost something of his nerve.

It has been claimed that Huarte was, to judge by his *Examen*, a man of saintly character, knowing no kind of hatred or envy. Although this is certainly the dominant impression afforded by his work, his natural good will was undeniably taxed by the bigoted criticism levelled against him. In the prologue to the new edition, he gently reminds the reader that man's congenital infirmity precludes the possibility of absolute certainty: "And thus I conclude, most curious reader, confessing openly that I am ill and distempered (and that you may also be the same) . . ." (p. 425). The signs of strain become more apparent in the revised opening chapters of his work. He laments that the *Examen* "has been examined and scrutinized by so many tribunals . . ." (p. 436), and records the reasons for the public's adverse reactions. He had claimed that some people were lacking all wit, whereas others were either without memory or without understanding. His work "informed the positivist [Scholastic] that his discipline was governed by the memory . . . ; [and informed] the distinguished lawyer that he could not possibly know how to govern" (p. 436). Moreover, certain of his readers had looked for their kind of wit, failed to find it, and were thereby annoyed. And, finally, "people said many other slanderous things . . ." (p. 436). Huarte's sorrow and anger turn to bitterness, as he notes that a little learning makes the fool more foolish.

Subsequent history has well justified Huarte's reaction, for it was only with the publication of Ildefonso Martínez's edition of the *Examen* in 1846 that his work was to appear again in Spain in an unexpurgated form. By this time, of course, the Inquisition had ceased to exist. In Italy the *Examen* remained completely banned until the Indices of the Catholic Church were recently suppressed.

III   *Some Modern Approaches*

In view of the reception accorded the *Examen* in his own day, Huarte would hardly have been surprised at the kind of critical turmoil that has surrounded his work in the modern period. Divergence of interpretation and violently impassioned discussion are the commonplaces of recent Huartean scholarship. The reasons are not hard to find. The vital nature of the issues in which the physician engaged and the continuing relevance of his ideas naturally make objective appraisal a difficult task. Moreover, his guarded manner of expression when dealing with thorny issues has not helped, for, however advisable in the context of Inquisitorial Spain, such a manner undeniably neutralizes the general clarity and precision of his style and exposition.

The interpretation of Huarte as a materialistic unbeliever, forced by precarious circumstances in a repressive society to dissimulate his views, undoubtedly appealed to the sensibility of the nineteenth century. It was expounded at great length, for example, by J. M. Guardia, who portrays Huarte as a brilliantly creative talent, smothered by an environment hostile to unorthodox views and misrepresented by Spanish scholars determined to see in him "a perfectly orthodox Christian, a good Catholic, a believer with a burning, immaculate faith."[5] For Guardia, Huarte's protestations of faith were precautionary measures, intended to deceive an organization with an unfailing nose for the heretical. The author of the *Examen* is "clearly deterministic" insofar as he follows the materialistic and atheistic views of Gómez Pereira, tends to deny the spirituality of the soul, and maintains that morality is explicable in physical terms.[6] His work was mutilated by the Inquisitors, and then neglected by Spanish scholarship.[7]

Spanish scholars have varied in their attitude to Huarte. At the other extreme to Guardia, Ildefonso Martínez y Fernández took the view that the *Examen* was perfectly orthodox and that the Inquisition was misguided in its interpretation of it: ". . . even today there is no work in the literary world in which religious and moral sentiments are more consonant with the achievements of science. . . ."[8] This approach to the *Examen* was followed by Mariano de Rementería, who made a special point of defending the orthodoxy of Huarte's claims concerning the interaction between matter and the spirit.[9] More recently it has been followed by Rodrigo Sanz, who, though admitting Huarte's support of a "subtle determinism,"[10] yet claims that the physician had merely stated that the immortality of the soul could not be demonstrated by induction, which is, in Sanz's view, an unexceptional standpoint. Sanz also asserts that to claim the understanding is organic is not a contradiction of any specific Christian dogma. In short, Huarte's critics were merely responding to "an ill-defined fear of scientific novelty."[11] Similarly, Francisco Salinas Quijada protests the absolute orthodoxy of the *Examen* and presents Huarte as a profoundly religious man, subjected "incomprehensibly" to persecution by the Inquisition.[12] Proof of such orthodoxy, in Quijada's view, is the fact that Huarte's daughter became a nun and that Huarte himself protested the sincerity of his faith.

Some scholars, while inclined to stress Huarte's sincerity of faith, have conceded his lack of complete orthodoxy to a limited degree. Jaime Salvá, for example, praises the *Examen* but regrets that Huarte should have introduced into his work "certain paradoxes";[13] and Antonio Hernández Morejón likewise qualifies his support.[14] Possibly even more conciliatory is M. de Iriarte. The extreme views of Guardia are "a pretext to vent his bitter, anti-Spanish sentiments."[15] The Spanish physician, Iriarte believes, possessed a "sincere religiosity,"[16] and was basically orthodox. However, forced by his scientific integrity to see mind and body as closely tied, Huarte "carefully weighs his words, so as to save both truths."[17] The errors in the *Examen* are thus largely of a linguistic nature, that is, "more in the manner of expression than in what is said,"[18] but to the extent that its author erred, "the intervention of the Inquisition was certainly not

unjust . . . ."[19] In any case, Iriarte concludes, the Inquisition left
unimpaired the basic framework of Huarte's views and that part
of his work that was most valuable. Similarly, Luis Rey Altuna
stresses Huarte's orthodoxy and underplays the idiosyncratic
aspects of the *Examen*: ". . . it is only incumbent upon us to ad-
judge the minor flaws in an innovatory doctrine, in the light of
constructive criticism."[20] He is a little annoyed with Huarte for
not making more of the Aristotelian-Scholastic solution to the
problem of the relationship between the soul and the body.

Also less extreme but, in comparison with the above scholars,
more inclined to Guardia's standpoint, are Gregario Marañón
and Arturo Farinelli. Marañón is convinced that Huarte was unwittingly but undeniably heretical in his views: "Because it is
clear that his soul was caught up in the theological unease of the
age. And that, even when he was fighting under the banner of
Catholic orthodoxy, his innermost being was infected by the great
corrosive virus of heresy, which engulfed some as in a hurricane,
whereas it undermined the unquestioning faith of others,
gradually and silently and without their realizing it."[21] He claims
some of Huarte's commentators have been wrong in seeing the
sections cut by the Inquisition as innocent. The Inquisition well
knew what it was about and had a keen eye for the potential
heretic. Inadvertently, Huarte arrived at standpoints incompatible with orthodoxy by following the logic of his views and apply-
ing with rigor methods that he believed to be the best.

Farinelli, though he maintains that the Inquisition left the
substance of the *Examen* intact,[22] also insists that Huarte was
more concerned with following science than the dogmas of the
Church. Without subtle dialectic or recourse to faith, Huarte
could never have supported the theory of the immortality
of the soul.[23] And the deterministic bias of Huarte's views
are undeniable: "What we find most disturbing [in the
Examen] . . . is the desire to harmonize the deterministic theory
of corporeal omnipotence with spontaneity [of behavior] in man
and his free will, so miserably circumscribed that we can hardly
recognize it as being alive and active. To save himself from
danger, it would have been necessary to be able to bring to bear a
titanic ratiocinative strength which the author of the *Examen* did
not possess. . . ."[24]

The *Examen* has thus proved susceptible to the wide variety of conflicting interpretation one would normally associate only with a work of imaginative literature. One is bound to insist, however, that the ultimately inescapable ambiguity of Huarte's own words is no excuse for the highly prejudiced nature of many of the contributions to Huartean scholarship.

CHAPTER 3

The Flight from Doubt

A T the time when Huarte was researching into those problems
that he would try to solve in the *Examen*, European scholarship was undergoing a crisis of skepticism. Luther's questioning of
ecclesiastical authority, during a period when classical skepticism
was being rediscovered in the West, opened a Pandora's box, and
soon scholars in other areas of knowledge and investigation were
critically reconsidering their basic assumptions and procedures.[1]
Given the nature of his discipline, with its dubious empirical
basis, and the rigorous manner of his inquiry, Huarte was bound
to be affected by the current skeptical trends. In turn, however,
he developed his own interest in methodology, so intimately en-
twined in the texture of his arguments, to an extent that suggests
that his individual contribution to the development of skeptical
thought in the Renaissance has not been sufficiently recognized.

One subject that particularly fascinated Huarte, as befitted a
scholar intending to throw light upon human psychology, was the
creative process by which he himself constructed his theories. He
indicates that the question that prompted his research into the
cause of men's natural inequalities in intellectual pursuits was
suggested by his personal experience of the disparity in his own
and his fellow students' performance in different subjects (p. 72).
His first step was to isolate the problem area, and to explore its
different facets. He consulted the relevant authorities on the subject of men's natural inequalities but found them singularly
unrevealing: "No philosopher, ancient or modern, that I have
read, has touched upon this difficulty, unnerved, so it seems to
me, by its great complexity, although I see them all critical of
men's conflicting judgments and appetites" (p. 419).

After a close observation of reality and with facts gleaned from
his reading, he set his mind to elaborate certain theories that
would answer the questions he had posed: ". . . I found it

necessary to let my mind soar and to make use of my inventive spirit, as with other, even greater problems that have as yet not begun to be solved" (p. 419). A method of procedure is clearly adumbrated at one point: we should "study science in a systematic manner, by beginning with [the] [basic] precepts, [and] rise through the intermediary stages to the end, without considering anything which presupposes [a knowledge of] other, as yet unexamined, material" (p. 77). His basic axiomatic assumptions included the equality of men's souls and the immortality of the soul: he seems rather naively unaware of the extent to which his work in general rested on theoretical categories derived from traditional science. The elaboration of a theory, Huarte assures us, is necessarily a demanding task, for truth does not surrender itself easily. The process involves constant "doubting and questioning," and indeed, by continually querying a master's conclusions, pupils themselves can teach him a good deal (p. 76). During this stage, quiet meditation, extended if necessary over years, is vital, with the problems, facts, and tentative solutions being turned over together in the mind, sometimes, Huarte seems to imply, at a subconscious level. Huarte is particularly insistent on the importance of this incubatory stage, claiming that the man of letters should:

". . . devote much time to studying and wait for knowledge to be digested and fully absorbed, for just as a body does not function on large quantities of food and drink ingested in a single day, but on what is [previously] broken down and digested in the stomach, so our understanding does not fatten on a vast amount read in a short time, but on what we reflect upon and understand gradually. Our mind is sharpened more and more each day, and, during the course of time, it comes to discover things it was previously unable to grasp or understand"(p. 77).

Here he seems to sense the existence of dark recesses of the mind, where thought processes are carried out of which we are but dimly, if at all, aware.[2] Eventually, if one is assiduous and persevering, Huarte suggests, the mind will yield its fruits. The result will not be perfect, for man is an imperfect creature and is incapable of attaining Truth, but the community of scholars, by their joint efforts, can perfect their theories, and each generation add a little to the total sum of human knowledge: ". . . in order that the sciences expand and achieve greater perfection, it is necessary to add the new discoveries of those of us now alive to what our predecessors left preserved in their books; because in this way the arts will progress, each one in its own time, and future generations will enjoy the discoveries and fruits of labor of those who preceded them" (p. 131). We should not ridicule the ideas of our forebears, Huarte protests, invoking the authority of Aristotle, least of all those of the inventors of sciences (of whom he sometimes considered himself to be an example), because their contribution, though superseded, is or was invaluable; and we should remember, he continues, that to add to an already established discipline is much easier than the task of actually establishing one (p. 68). Such a view of learning certainly allowed Huarte to explain his own inadequacies to posterity, but also sprang from deeply held beliefs, shared by some of his eminent contemporaries, about the nature and development of science.[3]

Huarte's insights into the psychological processes involved in intellectual speculation and his vision of the cumulative nature of scientific inquiry are undoubtedly fascinating, but they suggest in their own right (Huarte was himself the first to realize this) certain fundamental problems concerning the status of scientific knowledge. Indeed, from the beginning these problems threatened to paralyze his whole research program. Mature reflections led him to doubt the reliability of sense impressions as he came to realize the implications of his theory of the temperament. As he himself confesses in the prefatory material to the new revised edition of his work, all men are born "distempered" or unbalanced in mind and body, though they may not realize the nature of their defects and infirmity. The imbalance is not generally serious enough to be classified literally as an illness, requiring the attention of a doctor, but it is sufficient to cause a divergence of opinion among men. The faculties of the mind could function perfectly if they were entirely separate from the material world, which in fact they are not, insofar as they are dependent on the senses, which are in turn influenced by matter. Huarte explains:

Let us imagine, then, four men with defective powers of sight, and that one has a drop of blood obscuring the crystalline humor, another a drop of choler, another of phlegm, and another of melancholy. If we were to place before these men, who are (let us suppose) unaware of their illness, a piece of blue cloth and ask them to say what was its true color, it is certain that one would say it was red, another yellow, the third white, and the fourth black. And each would swear that he was right, and would ridicule the others for erring over such a plain, straightforward matter. And if we were to imagine these drops of humors transposed to the men's tongues and give them a jug of water, one would say it was sweet, another bitter, another salty, and another acidic.

You see here four different views, relating to two senses, for the simple reason that each one had its own particular distemper, and neither hit upon the truth. (p. 421)

According to Huarte, the material world conditions the human body, and in turn somatic changes cause corresponding changes in the psyche. In a sense, therefore, all men are insane, moving within the phantoms of their own creation: ". . . this world is no more than a mad-house, in which life is an amusing theatrical play performed to make men laugh . . ." (p. 422). Truth, for Huarte, would therefore only be attainable in a case where a perfect balance of the elements, and hence of the temperament, was achieved, for all men would then have the same concepts. This ideal situation was lost, however, at the Fall.

There can be no doubt that Huarte was deeply troubled by diversity of opinion among the learned, particularly that which he encountered when he had recourse to the work of other scholars in quest of answers to the issues that had come to attract his curiosity. Also disturbing was the fact that his own work did much to bring into question the axiomatic status of the very premises he himself initially adopted as the basis of his investigation. The reason for such chaos he found in the inherent weakness of the understanding: ". . . it must be admitted that, although the understanding is the most noble, most lofty, of man's faculties, there is none that is so easily deceived in the search for truth" (p. 217). Huarte believed that errors were bound to arise as the understanding, and indeed the imagination, endeavored to establish its own abstract constructs, and on reflection he found it natural that there should be so much disagreement among leading philosophers, doctors, theologians, and lawyers:

. . . the truth to be contemplated by the understanding, if not formulated and shaped by this faculty itself, has no formal being of its own; its materials are scattered and loose like a house reduced to a mass of bricks, earth, wood, and tiles, whose reconstruction could involve, through men's faulty imaginations, as many errors as there are individuals undertaking it. The same is true of the edifice the understanding constructs when framing truth, because, with the exception of the man of sound wit, people will make a thousand stupid mistakes, though they start from the same basic principles. (p. 218)

Huarte's previous portrayal of the progress of science seems but a dull echo as he bleakly portrays the chaotic stagnation of man's intellect:

Because men are not aware of the sad condition of their understanding, they dare to offer their opinions confidently, without knowing for certain what kind of wit they have and if it reasons well or badly. And, if the reader is not convinced, let us take some men of letters who, after having committed themselves in writing and supported their opinion with many arguments and proofs, have later changed their standpoint, and let us ask them when and how they will be able to know they have hit upon the correct formulation. As regards the first occasion, they themselves confess they were in error, since they retract what they said then. As regards the second, I believe they should show less confidence in their understanding, because the faculty that framed truth badly once, when its owner was so confident of its arguments and proofs, is open to the suspicion that it can err again, for the same reason, especially since experience has shown that a man can hold a correct view initially and later surrender it for another inferior, less probable one. (pp. 218–19)

Men blithely assume that, because their understanding is attracted to such and such an argument, there are good reasons for accepting it as correct, but, Huarte suggests, they are deceived in this. In essential respects the understanding resembles the lower faculties, for in the same way as different men are persuaded by different arguments, so they find different types of food appetizing. Some like meat cooked so rare that it is still running with blood, whereas others like it burned to a cinder. This is true of men who are healthy. Needless to say, Huarte adds, a man who is ill may prefer to eat earth than trout.

Variety of taste is not limited to food. The physician draws our attention to men's attitudes toward women, how some prefer ugly women to beautiful, foolish to intelligent, skinny to plump, and bedraggled to elegantly attired. And when we consider matters of preference regarding tangible qualities, what diversity do we find! Huarte elaborates the parallel with the intellect:

And this variety of strange tastes and appetites is found in the concepts that the understanding frames. For if we gather together a hundred men of letters and put a particular problem to them, each one will come to his own conclusion, and reason in a different way. One and the same argument seems fallacious to one, probably correct to another, and will totally convince a third. And this is not true merely with respect to different intellects, for experience shows that the same proof will convince a man at one time but not at another. Thus we see men change their views every day. Some men refine their intellect with the passing of time, and recognize the mistaken reasoning that moved them before; whereas others, because the temper of their brain is disturbed, come to hate truth and accept what is false. (p. 220)

Of course, if a man falls ill, his judgment becomes completely unreliable. He is convinced by weak arguments, and finds strong ones faulty. From the correct premises he derives the wrong conclusion, and imaginatively defends absurd views:

When intelligent, learned men realize this, they attempt to present their conclusions without the reasoning upon which these are based. Men are persuaded that an authoritative manner counts for as much as the logic of their views, and, since proofs are so indecisive, on account of the variety of men's understanding, each person evaluates truth according to the nature of his own particular intellect. Thus, it is generally considered more impressive to say "I believe this for certain reasons," than to explain the reasons upon which one bases one's judgment. But when a man is forced to explain his ideas, he draws upon all possible proofs, however trivial they may be, because the weakest proof turns out to be more persuasive than the one that is objectively the most sound. This highlights the poverty of our understanding, which composes, analyzes, argues, and reasons, and when all is said and done, lacks any definite means of knowing which opinion is correct. (pp. 220–21)

Huarte confesses that theologians suffer from the same problems as other scholars with respect to those matters that do not relate directly to faith, though their errors, lacking any basis in empirical fact, are less easily exposed. In contrast, the realm of faith is completely immune to the weakness of the understanding: "There can be no error in what the Church teaches in matters of faith, for God did not allow them to be dependent upon human reason. He knew how uncertain this reason is and how easily men are deceived . . . But in areas where the understanding has freedom to act, there is no possible way we can know which reasons are adequate or when the understanding successfully discovers the truth" (pp. 221–22).

Huarte was obviously sympathetic to a great extent to the view, often expressed by sixteenth-century skeptical philosophers such as his fellow-countryman Sánchez the Skeptic, that the very existence of varied opinions among learned men is a powerful argument for questioning man's rationality. Nevertheless, there is a certain laziness implicit in such a stance which was highly repellent to a man like Huarte, passionately absorbed as he was in many scientific problems which he felt, intuitively, to be anything but a fabric of fantasies and illusions. One possible solution to the skeptical dilemma clearly occurred to him while he was engaged in discussing the weaknesses of the understanding. He quotes approvingly Aristotle's comment that "the senses are always right" (p. 217). This reliability stems from the fact that "the objects of the five senses, and the entities with which they deal, are things real, firm, and stable by nature, which exist independently of man" (pp. 217–18). Speaking of the shortcomings of the understanding, he notes: "The five senses are immune to these errors and varied opinions, insofar as the eyes do not make the color, taste does not produce the flavors, and touch does not create the tangible qualities. Everything is made and composed by nature, before a person becomes acquainted with an object"(p. 218).

There was a problem here, however, that could not be sidestepped; for science, as Huarte was aware, consisted of more than mere observation and fact-finding. It is significant that, when discussing the discipline of medicine, Huarte should contrast those ancient and modern doctors who were very learned in theory and had a good knowledge of man in the abstract with the classical empiricists, who concentrated on the individual, in concrete situations. Both groups, says Huarte, are misguided, for medicine consists of both thought and experience. A doctor must have a good command of theoretical medicine, coupled with an intuitive knowledge gained from having seen and treated a large number of patients:

And thus it is a fact that the doctor's art consists of two things, which are as necessary for his task as two legs are necessary to walk without a limp. The first is to know by heart the precepts and rules for curing man in general, without reference to the particular; the second is to have actually practiced medicine for a long time, and to be able to recogize a great number of symptoms at a glance. Men are not so different that they do not resemble each other in many respects, nor so alike that they are not distinguished by particularities of their condition which cannot be explained, documented, taught, or systematized. A knowledge of such particularities is given only to those people who have often seen them and dealt with them. (p. 229)

Without a theoretical basis, observation will lack direction and coherence, but we should never forget that, since abstract scientific concepts are created by man, they do not partake of the perfection of God's creations (pp. 427–28) and need to be constantly weighed against fact.

Huarte realized that it is not merely the inherent insufficiency of both observation and abstract speculation, when each is pursued in isolation, that is troublesome. The philosopher must also consider how it is possible in practice to bridge the gap between theory and fact. This problem was particularly apparent when Huarte came to discuss the lack of empirical basis in his own subject of psychology: ". . . what shall we say of the discipline in which we are engaged, wherein the understanding anatomizes a subject so obscure and difficult as that concerning the powers and capacities of the rational soul? For it is plagued by so many doubts and uncertainties that there exists no body of generally accepted teaching on which to base one's work" (p. 134).

Huarte's quest for a criterion of truth was indeed a desperate one, and it is to his credit that in this situation he shunned facile solutions. He was certainly tempted by that intuitive sense of the rightness of a particular view, a certain balance ("buena consonancia") which convinces one that here lies truth. Yet ultimately his intellectual honesty asserted itself: ". . . and this is an argument that can deceive, for many things that are false often have the appearance of truth and of being easier to substantiate than things that are really true" (p. 222).

Some theories can be tested empirically, but, Huarte argues, this is true only with respect to certain disciplines, such as medicine and military strategy, in which theories stand or fall by their practical success in healing patients or in defeating the enemy. Furthermore, as he also explains, the complexity of events involved in particular situations suggests a basic inadequacy in this pragmatic criterion. There are so many unknown factors, so many variables, that make control and regulation impossible (p. 222).[4] Indeed, Huarte was so sensitive to the complexity of those disciplines that are bound up inextricably with physical reality that at times he looked on mathematics with some envy: ". . . natural philosophy is not based on such firm principles as the mathematical sciences . . ." (p. 138). He believed it was in fact inevitable that errors of judgment should occur in medicine and natural philosophy, and that this was not a comment upon their practitioners, as would be the case in mathematics. To err in the empirical sciences was human.

Huarte found entirely suspect Aristotle's view that a majority verdict provides a criterion of truth, "because as far as intellectual force is concerned, quality is preferable to quantity . . ." (p. 222). Discovering truth, he insists, is not to be compared to lifting a weight, in which the number of people involved is crucial. In matters of the mind one superb intellect is worth a thousand mediocre ones.

Socratic skepticism was naturally something with which Huarte was intimately familiar: "One of the reasons why the wisdom of Socrates has been celebrated down to the present day is that, after having been judged by the Oracle of Apollo to be the wisest man in the world, he spoke as follows: *hoc unum scio, me nihil scire*. All those people who have read these words and understood them believe that they were pronounced by Socrates because he was a most humble man, who despised human things and held all divine things to be of little value or foundation" (p. 133). The author of the *Examen* distinguishes carefully between Christian humility and Socratic doubt, maintaining that the latter springs from an intense awareness of the uncertainty of human reason: "What Socrates meant and gave to understand was what little certainty the sciences have, and how troubled and hesitant is the mind of a philosopher regarding all he knows, as he comes to see through experience that all is full of doubts and contradiction, and that he cannot commit himself to any view without fearing the opposite may be true . . ." (p. 133).

Yet, as we have seen, Huarte was instinctively repulsed by the negativeness of skepticism, and evinced a certain impatience with the seemingly intractable issues of methodology. For a man like himself, totally absorbed by scientific inquiry and the problems suggested by daily experience, such pessimism was uncongenial and insufficient to turn him from his pursuits. He therefore urges the scientist (and his words, one suspects, were aimed as much at himself as at anyone) to remain undaunted in his endeavor: ". . . he must be firm and steadfast, without fear or suspicion lest he be deceived; and the philosopher who does not proceed thus may truly say and claim that nothing can be known" (p. 134). Huarte was indeed one of the first scholars to begin to attack the contemporary skeptical philosophies and attempt to rescue human knowledge from the dark forces which threatened it. He

felt passionately that science, old and new, had attained a
measure of truth, and that its achievements must in the end
counterbalance any radical doubt. He seems, therefore, ultimately to have accepted the philosophical validity of skeptical
claims that we can attain no unquestionable truth, while at the
same time remaining convinced that we can, less ambitiously,
discover probable truths. In his discussion of methodology,
Huarte strove to do no more than to temper the skeptical standpoint and suggest certain useful methods of inquiry and procedure regarding his own discipline. For despite his theoretical
bent, he was also very practical in his outlook, and fully accepted
the need for knowledge of a pragmatic kind which would allow
us to get along in the everyday world.

To begin with, Huarte never surrendered his belief in the value
of empiricism, always asserting the need to study concrete reality
rather than accept the word of authority and books: ". . . the
prudence, wisdom, and truth contained in the sciences is sown,
according to Aristotle, in natural things, and in these it is to be
sought. . . . For truth is not to be found in the mouths of those
who expound science . . ." (pp. 428–29). This accounts for the
intensely personal character of the *Examen*, epitomized in such
phrases as "we know from experience," "I, as an eyewitness, can
affirm that it is so," "I discovered, of my own accord," etc., and
the innumerable examples that he draws from his own daily
observation of phenomena which he is analyzing.

Moreover, the correspondence between the macrocosm and the
microcosm, that is, between the universe and man, suggested a
methodological key with which Huarte tried to unlock the secrets
of man's inner being. The macrocosm *is* amenable to empirical
investigation, and, by drawing the necessary parallels, the
microcosm can be revealed. Hence the importance of such comments by Huarte as: ". . . the [understanding] functions, in
respect of the intellect, like the hobble we tie around the feet of a
difficult mule. The latter, after being hobbled for a few days,
begins to walk with a certain ease of movement . . ." (p. 74).[5]
Wherever even this tenuous connection with empirical fact is absent, as in the "divine sciences," which "do not make use of the
senses," an exceptional clarity of intellect is required (p. 430).
Huarte himself was obviously too attached to empirical fact to
feel at ease in such areas, and indeed was to elaborate a
philosophy of double-truth which excluded these nonempirical

subjects from "science" defined as the *rational* inquiry into nature. Unfortunately, his empiricism also seems to have blinded him to the importance of mathematics in scientific research.

Huarte was also anxious to warn against the false currency of language, and to encourage men to turn their attention to natural phenomena. He believed that a healthy nominalism should characterize scientific speculation, and that we use a term such as *instinct* merely to hide our ignorance, thereby blinding ourselves to the need for further scientific elaboration (p. 100). His work thus continues the Humanistic distrust of Scholastic abstraction and anticipates the seventeenth-century conviction that language does not adequately reflect reality. Like the new men of science, he was impatient with the inflated eloquence that had sometimes characterized Humanistic scholarship, which he saw as masking the essential simplicity and order of the Creation. The orators' indifference to truth was their greatest sin: ". . . they defended the view that it was better to be poor than rich, better to be ill than healthy, and better to be foolish than wise. . ." (p. 181). They were content merely to impress: ". . . [the orator] knew only the superficialities and established maxims of all [the sciences], without understanding fundamentally the rationale and aims of any" (p. 198). However, not for the one and only time, Huarte's ideas contain contradictions. His conviction of the need to define adequately one's terminology, though in itself good advice in the interests of scientific rigor, led him insidiously into the trap against which he had so carefully warned others. In his discussion of the meaning of "ingenio," for example, he delves at length into the etymology of the word in quest of some mysterious essence (p. 426).

Finally, Huarte optimistically maintained that a man may discover truth in the area in which, as a result of the imbalance of his faculties, he individually excels: "We should remember that a man never suffers from an illness without the weakening of one faculty occasioning thereby the strengthening of another" (p. 424). Hence he believed that the Humanists excelled in the faculty of memory, and surrendered to a fascination with the "ornament of words" at the expense of the understanding, "whose task is the *fundamental* pursuit of truth" (p. 183). Alternatively, in other individuals, there is a weakening of the memory, matched by a hypertrophy of the understanding. In practice, therefore, the *destemplado* ("distempered") surpasses the *templado* ("tempered"), for, once he knows the nature of his illness, a man can apply himself accordingly, attaining truth in his favored science while continuing perhaps to speak nonsense in the others.

To conclude, Huarte overcame his initial crisis, and was able to proceed with his work. The skepticism remained as an undercurrent, encouraging a healthy concern with the evaluation of evidence but never being sufficient to restrain unduly his creative urge or smother his enthusiasm. The standpoint he adopted resembles closely that held by most modern philosophers of science. It is now generally accepted that science does not depend upon some unshakable system, and that all its constructs are ultimately open to doubt. At the same time, however, it is maintained that its cumulative achievements are in themselves a powerful defense against skepticism.

CHAPTER 4

The Sources

INTELLECTUALLY, Huarte was affiliated with a small but eminent group of sixteenth-century natural philosophers, which included such figures as Paracelsus, Bruno, and Montaigne. They were united by little more than a desire to deepen our understanding of the world, a tendency to emphasize their own originality, and their advocacy of the direct study of nature.[1] Hence Huarte set out to investigate "natural things" (p. 428), presented himself as the "first inventor" of his discipline (p. 68), and affirmed that truth is to be found not in "authorities" but in "the object under investigation" (p. 429). Indeed, Huarte anticipated that the innovatory nature of his ideas would arouse resentment in some quarters. Addressing his reader, he writes: ". . . if your wit is of the vulgar, common kind, I am well aware you are persuaded that the correct number of sciences already exists and that they reached a state of perfection long ago in the time of the Ancients; for you wrongly assume that, because the Ancients had nothing more new to say, originality in the sciences is impossible" (p. 65). Huarte himself rather immodestly promises to produce conclusions that "because of their newness are worthy of great admiration" (p. 65).

However, both he and his fellow natural philosophers undoubtedly exaggerated their claims to originality, for in certain respects their work was *fundamentally* derivative with regard to traditional scholarship. Up to a point this was the result of accepting without question certain "common sense" concepts which were in fact highly sophisticated, if misguided, traditional views. It is clear that Renaissance scholars were commonly not aware of the extent to which many of the terms they used were "theory-laden." In Huarte's case his attempt to cast himself in the role of the initiator of his discipline is not only belied by his considerable indebtedness to the work of his predecessors, but is also contradicted by his incremental view of the development of science.

A careful consideration of the *Examen* certainly confirms the approach to the Renaissance that stresses the complexity of its cultural movements and the extent of its intellectual ferment, as opposed to the approach that attempts simplistically to define the Renaissance in terms of the triumph of a particular philosophical trend; for there is hardly one leading school of thought, ancient or medieval, that has not left its trace in Huarte's work. Despite the fact that he probably had no knowledge of Greek, and only a serviceable command of Latin, Huarte shows himself to be well versed in classical thought. His four major sources are Plato, Aristotle, Galen, and Hippocrates. Lesser, though not unimportant, influences are Cicero and Quintilian. He was also well read in Christian philosophy, particularly St. Augustine and St. Thomas Aquinas, and of course the Scriptures figure prominently in his work.[2]

One cannot always be certain whether Huarte took his material directly from its original source, or incorporated it via some secondary source—St. Augustine, for instance, was the door through which much classical learning passed into Europe. Influences could be even more indirect than this, however, operating via their incorporation into the prevailing world view of the age, which to a great extent Huarte shared. Huarte's independence of viewpoint is apparant in the care and discrimination with which he evaluates received opinion. Though clearly comforted by the support he finds in "authorities," he never hesitates to express his own ideas and reject what seems to him to be misguided in other scholars, no matter how eminent they may be.

I   *Galen and Hippocrates*

Classical medical theory influenced Huarte in two ways: by providing, firstly, the basic physiological doctrine of the *Examen*, and, secondly, an important model for scientific procedure. Medical theory in antiquity is associated with two names: Hippocrates and Galen. The collection of medical writings known as the Hippocratic Corpus was the work of a large number of writers between 430 and 330 B.C. It consists of about sixty anonymous treatises, differing not only in subject matter and style but also in their views of the aims and methods of science. Little is known for certain about Hippocrates himself, or the extent of his own role in the production of the Corpus. Born probably in 460 B.C. on the island of Cos, he came of a family of physicians and was closely associated with a medical school on the island which produced many talented doctors. He had the reputation of being a calm, retiring, thoughtful man. The second giant of classical medicine was Galen (c. A.D. 130–c. 200) of Pergamum. In his youth Galen visited Alexandria and other centers of learning, but later went to Rome where he remained for virtually the rest of his life. He achieved a great biological and medical synthesis of classical doctrine which was accepted in its broad outline until Versalius in the sixteenth century. Galen's pervasive influence (indicated parenthetically below) is felt throughout the *Examen*, a fact which makes imperative a full understanding of the Galenic system in the analysis of this work.[3]

A. *The Frame of Man*

Classical medical theory viewed the physiological function of the complex human organism as being that of adapting external pneuma or air to the three grades of life in man: these being growth (shared with plants), movement (shared with animals), and reason (by which man is unique) (pp. 105–106). It was maintained that all mundane things are made up of four qualities: heat, dryness, humidity, and cold (pp. 99, 121), which generate in combination the four elements: air, water, earth, and fire (p. 343). Air is hot and wet; water is cold and wet; earth is cold and dry; and fire is hot and dry. The link between the physical universe and man's physical life begins with food, which is made up of the four elements (p. 344). Food passes through the stomach to the liver, which converts the food into four liquid substances, the humors, which are to the body what the elements are to the common matter of the world (pp. 123, 137, 230). Each humor has its own counterpart among the elements. Hence melancholy corresponds to earth, phlegm to water, blood to air, and choler to fire (pp. 137, 143). The qualities of the humors are naturally identical to those that correspond to the elements. When Huarte and his contemporaries used the word *temperament* they had in mind the tempering of one humor (or element, as they often said) by another, or the intermixing of the humors that was the cause of character (p. 87). If a man was of phlegmatic temperament, it meant the four humors were mixed in a way that allowed phlegm (the cold and moist humor) to dominate (p. 420). Besides these normal conditions of the humors, found in the healthy and sane, there were abnormal ones in which the excess of a humor reached clearly pathological proportions. Disease was generally seen as some kind of imbalance or disturbance of the natural state of the body (p. 419). Thus, the distemper of man's body is due to an excess of, say, heat, causing a fever, or of cold, causing a chill. In this way the cosmic system had repercussions in individual physiology.

In the liver, ingested food is turned into blood and imbued with a pneuma, the *natural spirits*, innate in all living substance while alive, and passed into the veins for the growth of the body. The motion of blood in the veins is a sluggish oscillation. The portal vein carries the blood from the liver to the right ventricle of the heart. Here it is parted from impurities, which are passed into the lungs, via the pulmonary artery, and exhaled. A portion of the purified blood passes via the septum into the left ventricle, where it meets again pneuma from the outer world conveyed to the left ventricle by the pulmonary vein. This second point of contact between human physiology and the cosmos enables scholars to argue the influence of the climate on man (p. 420). The air, taken into the lungs and passed on to the heart, enters the blood in the left ventricle and is elaborated into a higher pneuma, the *vital spirits* (pp. 149, 150). These are distributed throughout the body by the arteries. Some of the arteries lead to the brain (p. 246), passing through the network of vessels called the "rete mirabile." Here there is a third adaptation: a portion of the blood becomes endowed with *animal spirits* (pp. 118, 119) and is distributed throughout the body by the nerves, which are hollow.

The vital spirits are the link between the body and the soul (p. 97), the latter being located in the brain (p. 90 ff.). Man's soul, the seat of his higher faculties, is hierarchically organized into three divisions. The lowest contains the five senses; the middle contains the fancy, the memory, and the common sense; these three process impressions derived from the senses; and the third and highest division, which works upon the processed material from the second, contains the supreme human faculty of reason, made up of the understanding and will.

Though Huarte accepted this common tradition of ancient

medical theory in its fundamental respects, he did also alter and modify it. For example, not only did he simplify the psychical component into three major faculties (the understanding, memory, and imagination) (pp. 418–19), but argued that animals possess a kind of rational soul (p. 96). Moreover, while he accepted that Galen was very much indebted to the Hippocratic Corpus, Huarte saw differences of detail between the two great classical authorities which had very important repercussions, particularly as regards the crucial issue of the nature of the relationship between body and soul. According to his interpretation, Hippocrates, while conceding the importance of the balance of the four elements in man's physical and mental makeup, always avoided the view that the soul is conditioned directly by the body;[4] whereas Galen, following the spirit if not the letter of Hippocrates, maintained that the rational soul was governed strictly by the temperament.[5] Huarte certainly records his debt to Galen in no uncertain terms (". . . all that Galen wrote in his book [*De Placitis Hippocratis et Platonis*] is the basis of this work [the *Examen*] . . ." [p. 88]), but he also notes the objection by moral philosophers to Galen's view on the body-soul relationship, and is himself fully aware of its implications regarding free will (p. 440). It seems, as we shall see in more detail later, that, although he was obliged to agree that the orthodox Christian view was the correct one, Huarte found Galen's (and Hippocrates', to the extent that it agreed with Galen's) more consonant with his own materialistic tendencies.[6]

B. *Methodology*

I have suggested that classical medicine also influenced Huarte's methodological procedure. It is important to remember that in antiquity, as in the Renaissance, the boundaries between disciplines were much less clearly defined than they have become in the modern world. Not only was the realm of philosophy far broader than it is considered to be today, but practitioners of such disciplines as medicine did not hesitate to enter areas of abstract speculation. This symbiotic relationship was doubtless facilitated by the relative lack of any requisite technical or professional training in medicine. At all events, Huarte, like many of his Hippocratic predecessors, would have seen philosophical speculation as a natural extension of professional interest in medicine.

Although there was no single, dominant Hippocratic system, there were certain very general procedural methods associated with the Corpus, which had a largely beneficial effect on the development of Greek science, and, via such works as Huarte's *Examen*, on Renaissance science as well. Important contributions by Hippocratic writers to Greek science were made in four main areas. Firstly, their insistence on the importance of observation provided a healthy antidote to the excessively abstract bias of Greek science.[7] Huarte continued this emphasis on observation and its correlative skepticism toward "authorities." Less fortunately, perhaps, his *Examen* is also characterized by the Hippocratic dependence on a highly sophisticated physiological doctrine that contradicts the allegedly unflinching empiricism of his methodology.

Secondly, it would be true to say that the whole Greek notion of causation was originally refined in the context of medicine.[8] Greek medical practitioners helped encourage the tendency to eschew systematically all supernatural explanation of phenomena. They rejected, for example, the widespread view of epilepsy as the "sacred" disease, insisting that it could be diagnosed in the normal manner. We will see that Huarte continued these aspects of the Hippocratic tradition, expressing his distrust of the ostentatiously fantastic and mysterious while demanding that science be furthered via a strict adherence to rationalistic methods and an adequate notion of causation.

Thirdly, Greek doctors contributed decisively to a growing discussion of the relative importance of theoretical knowledge and its practical application. Whereas Greek thinkers were notably theoretical in outlook, doctors often stressed the practical application of knowledge.[9] Again, Huarte generally shared their bias, for, despite his attraction to theoretical discussion and his scorn for the manual arts, he was certainly of a practical outlook himself, and indeed wrote his *Examen* to suggest the desirability of certain specific reforms in education.

Finally, medical theory refined an analogical method of explantation which decisively influenced ensuing scientific speculation. As a fruitful means of suggesting hypotheses, analogy had been used from the very beginning of Greek science, but it was richly applied in medical theory from the fifth century, as doctors strove to overcome the problem of investigating vital but hidden processes within the body.[10] Huarte found analogical explanation invaluable in dealing with the most inaccessible area of man, namely, the mind. However, such a methodological tool was certainly not without its dangers, and Huarte continued the unfortunate tendency, too often apparent in Hippocratic writers, to mistake an analogy for a demonstration.

II *Plato*

Both Plato (c. 427–347 B.C.) and Aristotle (384–322 B.C.) were interested in medicine, and influenced Huarte in this respect. But it is on a more general, philosophical level that their impact on the *Examen* is most striking. Huarte refers to Plato (and the Platonic Socrates) in a wide variety of contexts. Sometimes he uses the authority of the philosopher merely to bolster his own views and prejudices regarding relatively trivial matters; whereas at other times his aim is to extend his analysis of central issues by a detailed examination of Plato's ideas. Hence Plato's name figures, for example, in Huarte's passing mention of the need for discrimination in the choosing of pupils (p. 64), and in his careful consideration of the key subject of "divine madness" (p. 433). However, the author of the *Examen* always maintains his independence of viewpoint, even to the extent of being critical. Plato's theory of innate knowledge, for example, is attractive to him, but ultimately he finds it untenable (pp. 71, 104), and the philosopher's insights regarding the nature of poetry, although suggestive, are too mystical and unscientific to satisfy the Spaniard in the form in which he expressed them (pp. 169–70).

In the development of Western philosophy, Platonic thought had undergone radical transformation and assumed various guises,[11] with the result that, although Plato's impact on Huarte is considerable, it is not always easy to ascertain the kind of influence we are dealing with in a particular case. Much of it, of course, was direct. The Platonic corpus was available after 1350, and Huarte had certainly read such works as the *Cratylus* in the Latin translation. Plato had also been known throughout the Middle Ages, however, and St. Augustine, with whom Huarte was familiar, was much influenced by his thought. Moreover, outside the universities in the second half of the fifteenth century, the philosophical scene came to be increasingly dominated by a new Platonic current, centered on the Florentine Academy. Its

most eloquent exponents were Marsiglio Ficino (1433–99) and
Giovanni Pico della Mirandola (1463–94). Ficino explained the
divinity of the soul in terms of man's fixed, unique position as the
vinculum mundi, whereas Plato argued that man's excellence lay
precisely in the fact that he had no clearly determined essence or
nature and could fashion his own destiny through the exercise of
will.[12] Wherever we turn in the Renaissance we discover echoes of
these themes. Nicholas Cusanus (c. 1400–1464), for example,
pointed to the likeness between the mind of man and God, and
maintained that just as God created the world, so man creates his
thoughts, thereby forming the arts and sciences. For Cusanus,
man's striving for the infinite is the seal of his divine origin.[13]
These ideas were popularized in the sixteenth century, and must
have been known to Huarte, who was himself to make a notable
contribution to the discussion of creativity.

III   *Aristotle*

Aristotle, though little known under the Romans, was the
dominating influence in Western philosophy from the twelfth
and thirteenth centuries on. An older view of the Renaissance saw
this age as one in which Plato dethroned his pupil, but more recent scholarship has stressed the continuity of an Aristotelian
tradition in the sixteenth century,[14] and certainly, when we turn
to the *Examen*, it is Aristotle who is seen to figure more prominently. As with Plato, Huarte's references are sometimes
fleeting, usually to add weight to his own personal view. For example, he shared Aristotle's disapproval of criticism of the in-
itiators of a science (p. 68), and found helpful the philosopher's
comparison between the intellectual capacities of man and the
animals (pp. 95–96). Other references to Aristotle, however, are
more central, as when Huarte draws extensively on his views concerning the workings of the mind and body (pp. 134 ff.), the
nature of language (pp. 164–65), and the need to adopt empirical
procedures in science (pp. 428–29).

It is not always certain whether Huarte is drawing upon Aristotle directly, or being influenced by his later followers. His
knowledge of the Aristotelian concept of causation, for example,
may have been passed on to him via Scholasticism, or as a part of
the intellectual baggage of the contemporary educated man.

Similarly, he may have learned his empiricism from Pietro Pomponazzi (1462–1525) and other Italian Aristotelians, along with the desirability of separating science from theology. With these Aristotelians Huarte also shared a seriousness of intellectual commitment and a sense of the importance of a rigorously defined terminology.[15]

Huarte is never afraid to criticize Aristotle, when he thinks him misguided, as when the philosopher claims that all human knowledge is derived from sense impressions (p. 105), and when he dissociates the soul completely from the organic sphere (pp. 138–39). To this extent, therefore, Huarte shares also in the strong anti-Aristotelian trend in Renaissance thought, which recurs regularly from Petrarch to Galileo. It was only after Huarte, however, that the new men of science challenged the whole Aristotelian world view with an alternative system. Huarte, despite his originality, still moved within a largely Aristotelian universe.

IV *Augustinianism*

Irrespective of his possible role as the transmitter of Platonic thought, St. Augustine (354–430) was an important influence on Huarte. The physician was particularly influenced by Book IV of *De Doctrina Christiana*, in which St. Augustine contrasts the eloquence of words with the immeasurably greater eloquence of realities.[16] It was probably his reading of St. Augustine that confirmed Huarte's own attraction to an unpretentious, unsophisticated style, such as that in which the Scriptures had been composed (pp. 182–83). Like St. Augustine, he believed that eloquence, though it is useful to the Christian speaker, is not indispensable, for truth needs no ornament to give pleasure (p. 188 ff.).

Huarte seems also to have been familiar with the Augustinian view of creativity in the arts. For St. Augustine, God's excellence is manifested in the variety of things that He has created *ab initio*, in contrast to man, who can cause only contingent being and whose inferiority is shown in his limited ability to reproduce the diversity of natural objects in works of art. St. Augustine concludes, somewhat negatively and pessimistically, that those people who fashion these works, and indeed those who delight in them, are not to be highly esteemed. He believes, in other words, that God the Creator is *not* to be imitated, and that man should not employ his creative powers.[17] Such a view was known to Huarte, and was one that he utilized at some length in the revised edition of his work (pp. 427–28). As a general philosophy, however, it would scarcely have been congenial to him, insofar as he himself was committed to a decidedly optimistic view of human creativity.

V *Scholasticism*

Scholasticism, a philosophical movement which began in the twelfth century and whose aim was the incorporation of Aristotle ("the Philosopher") into Christian philosophy, continued to dominate the universities in the Renaissance, particularly in Spain. Not surprisingly, therefore, it left an unmistakable mark on the *Examen*. On a general level, Huarte found the seriousness of the Scholastics' commitment a refreshing contrast to the Humanists' superficial cult of rhetoric. He also admired their stylistically simple and uncluttered language as well as their indifference to the aesthetic dimension of Latin composition (pp. 166–67). More specifically, Huarte probably owed to Thomas Aquinas (1225–74) and Duns Scotus (1270–1308) his interpretation of Aristotle as the chief exponent of the *tabula rasa* view of the mind. It might also have been their influence that encouraged him to stress the creative activity of the mind, over and above the sense impressions which are the primary data of experience, and to define nature as an order of secondary causes, willed by God, who is the First Cause (pp. 84–85). Huarte may also have been guided in his discussion of the soul by Scotus's view that there are powerful arguments both for and against the immortality of the soul, and that Aristotle's teachings on the subject are confused.[18]

The Scholastic combination of theological and philosophical speculation achieved the status of official doctrine, continuing into and beyond the fourteenth century. However, a new movement grew up in the fourteenth century, associated to a great extent with William of Ockham (died c. 1349). It was both nominalist and empiricist in its tendencies, characterized by a growing separation between theology and philosophy.[19] Its obvious ties with the *Examen* remind us yet again of the dangers of exaggerating the originality of Renaissance movements.

VI *Humanism*

It is not easy to ascertain the extent of Huarte's connections with Humanism, a major current of Renaissance thought which began in Italy about the beginning of the fourteenth century and thereafter gradually spread over the rest of Europe. Some of his commentators have been anxious to dissociate him from this particular movement,[20] and, indeed, if we see its core interest as being the study of the Classics, rhetoric, poetry, and history, in conjunction with moral philosophy,[21] then it is true that Huarte was no Humanist. He felt for the most part a notable distaste for imaginative literature, and was decidedly amoral in his approach to learning. He was, moreover, instinctively opposed to the Humanistic cult of rhetoric and, despite his own skeptical leanings, opposed to their indifference to genuine wisdom (p. 183).

It would be wrong, however, to detach Huarte entirely from Humanism. On a superficial but not unimportant level, he was indebted to this movement for his knowledge of the Classics. The primary task of Humanists was to transcribe, comment upon, and make available a corpus of classical texts. They provided thereby an invaluable service since the ancient world still had much to teach the modern world in the fifteenth and early sixteenth centuries.[22] We shall see later that Huarte was also influenced by the Humanistic drive to refine pedagogical methodology.

As a literary movement, Humanism was basically non-philosophical, but where Humanists extended their area of concern they sometimes produced work with which Huarte would have been in sympathy. He would certainly have approved of the attack by Lorenzo Valla (1407–57) upon excessive abstraction in Scholastic terminology, and the nominalism and empiricism that fifteenth-century Humanists often encouraged is reflected in his own criticism of such notions as "actio" and "potentia."[23]

Paul Oskar Kristeller has pointed to the links between the Humanistic movement and a few notions or attitudes that are of potential philosophical significance.[24] Of these, two are of fundamental importance and relate to Huarte's work. They are, firstly, an increasingly exalted view of man, particularly with respect to his privileged position in the scheme of things, and, secondly, a greater concern with the individual self and his concrete experience of life. The glorification of man, of course, was by no means a new discovery of the Renaissance. It is often found in Greek literature and philosophy, and is implied in Genesis and in certain aspects of Christian thought. However, Christian thinkers traditionally emphasized man's fallen state, and it seems likely that it was in conscious opposition to this pessimistic vision that Humanists first emphasized man's excellence.[25] As we shall see, the *Examen* may be said to constitute a highly articulate elaboration of this Humanistic theme. As regards the Humanists' interest in the individual, we have already drawn attention to Huarte's almost obsessive concern with the workings of his own mind, and the freedom with which, in the pursuit of scientific truth, he draws upon personal experience. His discussion of the problem of immortality—obviously a ramification of the prevailing concern with the individual self—will be considered later.

VII   *Contemporary Influences*

The task of tracing the influence of contemporary works on Huarte is not an easy one, for the simple reason that, although he is very conscientious (for his times) in quoting his classical sources, it is his policy neither to quote nor to refer explicitly to any contemporary author. This does not mean, as some commentators have suggested, that Huarte lived in intellectual isolation, but merely that he followed the conventions of the age by not naming his contemporary sources. There are, in fact, numerous echoes of other Renaissance scholars in his work. One feels certain he must have read Luis Vives (1493–1540) and Pedro Simón Abril (born c. 1530), both men inspired with a reforming zeal in pedagogy comparable to his own, and also his fellow physician Gómez Pereira (born c. 1500), who speculated with equal originality on the nature of human and animal intelligence. Huarte must also have been very familiar with contemporary medical treatises and other works relating to his professional interests.

To conclude, the fact that Huarte was so indebted to traditional scholarship tends initially to give the impression that he was a mere eclectic devoid of original insights. And indeed it must be admitted that there are few important ideas in the *Examen* that, when considered in isolation, do not seem to derive from some particular source. The more we know about the ancients and medieval Christian philosophers, the more we may be inclined to ask ourselves what, if anything, was the product of

Huarte's own genius. His contemporaries, however, saw him as an innovator, and as a man who treated problems in a fresh and challenging way; and closer inspection indicates that their view is far from being without foundation. Huarte was eclectic only in the sense that he was open to ideas from a variety of sources, not in the sense that he was indifferent to truth or simplistic in his view of knowledge. He evaluated the views of other men with care, and rethought traditional material coherently and systematically. It is here that he shows his quality as a scholar. Above all, insofar as he undermined the medieval respect for authority, he made an important contribution to Western thought, one which had considerable repercussions.

CHAPTER 5

The Nature and Identity of Man

THE fact that Huarte has been praised by some scholars as the champion of human dignity, but was regarded in his own day as a potentially dangerous exponent of determinism, suggests a basic ambivalence in his attitude to man and an inescapable ambiguity in his vision of human nature. Convinced as he was of man's exalted status in the scheme of things, he was yet committed to a rationalistic, scientific methodology which had no place for such mysterious concepts as "freedom" and "creativity," on which man's claims to excellence rested. As a scientist Huarte was interested in abstracting regular patterns and consistencies from nature, thereby reducing the realm of the inexplicable.

The general context within which Huarte developed his theory of human nature was that of the Great Chain of Being. The metaphor of the Chain of Being embodies what was, until modern times, the prevailing view of the structure of the universe. It has its genesis in the basic Platonic division of the universe into two realms of other-worldliness and this-worldliness, but its full articulation was only achieved in Christian philosophy. During the course of time the notion of "degree" became more prominent, as each created thing assumed its place in a chain which stretched from God to the depths of hell. As a result, the system became increasingly anthropocentric. Man was deemed to partake of the spiritual and corporeal, to constitute thereby a little world, the microcosm, which contained within itself all the attributes of the universe, the macrocosm. Human anatomy corresponded, it was believed, with the physical hierarchy of the universe, the faculties of the mind, for example, being ordered according to their degree of excellence. The concept was adopted by the Alexandrian Jews, propagated by the Neoplatonists, and became one of the great commonplaces of

Western thought from the Middle Ages to the eighteenth century, pervading many diverse realms of scholarship.[1]

From the beginning the whole idea of a hierarchy was plagued by an ever-recurrent problem: the conflict between the desire of scholars for discrete classificatory units and certain of their notions that emphasized the "fullness" of creation. These notions were the Platonic principle of plenitude, according to which there existed in the world all conceivable kinds of living things; and the Aristotelian notion of the continuity of creation, which suggested the gradual merger between different organisms which constitute the hierarchy, with no clear lines of demarcation between each.[2] Such conflict was aggravated by the fact that, throughout the history of European culture, the dominant anthropocentric philosophy never passed completely unchallenged, although within the context of Christian culture an attack upon man's traditionally exalted state was always regarded as something of a heresy. The challenge to the anthropocentric tradition was strengthened in the Renaissance by the revival of skepticism, for one of the cherished traditional views increasingly questioned was that of man's supreme status in the creation.[3]

Though accepting man's unquestionably privileged place in the scheme of things, Huarte emphasizes the idea of the continuity of creation. He paraphrases Galen: ". . . the difference between man and the brute beasts is the same as that which exists between the fool and the wise man. [That is to say], it is merely one of degree" (p. 96). Galen had been obliged to carry out much of his dissection on the higher animals, and assume a parallel with man, which of course existed but which he exaggerated. Following this tradition, Huarte emphasizes the similarities between man and beasts. He maintains that animals possess memory, imagination, and a faculty that "resembles" the understanding, and that, though man has a larger brain than other animals, the ape, fox, and dog are not far removed from him as regards intelligence. Individual animals vary in ability like men: some asses, for example, are stupid, whereas others are so crafty "they transgress the bounds of their species" (p. 96).

However, it seems that, in terms of the Christian tradition, the *Examen* emphasized excessively the continuity of the Chain of Being. The Inquisition insisted on deletions (see pp. 380–82), and Huarte's own use of "resembled" when talking of the third faculty of animals indicates unease regarding either the validity of his view or its inevitable reception by the public.

Yet Huarte did accept the fact of man's preeminence and his excellence above all other creatures. He refers in passing to the traditional view of man as distinguished by his reason (p. 209), but the seemingly rational feats of animals possibly suggested to him that this was not a sufficiently distinctive attribute. Similarly, he notes that language is an exclusively human faculty (p. 95), but again fails to make much of the fact, possibly because he sees language as associated with the memory, the humblest of the faculties. In short, Huarte came to believe man's uniqueness rested on his creative wit, for "in this alone is man distinguished from the brute beasts . . ." (p. 435).

Huarte was persuaded not only of the importance of his concept of creativity, but also of its originality, finding it singularly absent from traditional theories of human knowledge. He summarizes succinctly the Platonic view that all knowledge is latent in the human soul, infused prior to its union with the body, and that rational discovery is basically nothing more than a species of "reminiscing": ". . . our rational soul is older than our body, because, before the latter was formed by nature, it was already in heaven, in the presence of God, whence it descended, replete with science and knowledge; but, on coming to inform matter, . . . it lost [this science and knowledge], until . . . little by little it remembered what it had forgotten" (p. 104). Similarly, he traces the alternative empirical view, which he sees as deriving from Aristotle, that all knowledge must ultimately originate in sense data, the human mind being no more than a *tabula rasa* at birth. He paraphrases Aristotle thus: "Everything men know and learn originates in what they hear, see, smell, taste, and touch, because there can be nothing in the understanding that was not first passed through one of the five senses" (p. 105). Both of these approaches are unsatisfactory in Huarte's view, since neither allowed for the role of human creativity. Aristotle's view suggested a passive *implanting* of knowledge; whereas Plato's view implied a revealing of what is already latent or contained within the mind.

Huarte's view of human nature was rather more complex than that implied by either of the above traditional standpoints, as he outlined them. As a student of pedagogical theory and practice, he found it necessary to distinguish three kinds of wit in man. The first kind is exhibited by those people who are superficial and un-creative, and lacking in imagination:

Some people show a natural ability in mastering the clear, easy notions of the art they are learning but, when it comes to those which are more pro-found and very delicate, the teacher tries in vain with good examples to make them reproduce an image; and, because they lack the capacity, they are unable to use their own imagination to invent their own image. Within this category fall those pathetic talents in any discipline, who, when consulted regarding the easy matters of their science, tell you everything it is possible to know, but, when it comes to the most delicate, they utter a thousand stupidities. (p. 130)

Men possessing the second kind of wit can learn by heart, but are incapable of active participation: "They are soft, and it is easy to impress in them all the rules and considerations of the art, whether these be clear, complex, easy, or difficult; but the doc-trine itself, the argument and counter-argument, the questions and distinctions, all this has to be given to them ready-made. Peo-ple of this kind need to assimilate the learning of good, knowledgeable teachers, to have a wide selection of textbooks, and to study ceaselessly, because the less they read and hear, the less they will know" (p. 130). It was this kind of people Aristotle had in mind when developing his *tabula rasa* view of the mind, "because everything they know and learn they must first hear from another, and are unable to use it inventively" (p. 130).

The third kind of wit encompasses those men who are truly creative: ". . . wits so perfect that they have no need of masters to teach them or tell them how to philosophize; because from one fact dictated by the professor, they derive a hundred; and without anything being said to them, their mouths are filled with science and learning" (pp. 130–31). These were the minds that deceived Plato into thinking knowledge was innate. Grouping the first two kinds of wit into one category, and contrasting it with the third, Huarte compares both groups respectively to sheep and goats. The sheep remain passively in the lowlands, whereas the goats, ever adventurous, leap across the rocky heights. Hence some men accept what they are told without question, whereas others indulge in creative thought. Only creative minds should be allowed to write books, claims Huarte, so that the sciences may progress.

In the revised edition of the *Examen* (1594), Huarte had second thoughts about the three kinds of wits and the whole notion of creativity, which he elaborates afresh at length. He criticizes Cicero and Aristotle for suggesting that man's wit is based on memory. Such a dependence, he argues, would exclude inventiveness and creativity, for the memory is inhibiting in this respect. The three basic kinds of wit remain, but their boundaries have shifted slightly. The second kind now includes some men who have a modicum of creative capacity (". . . inventing and uttering things they have never heard from their teachers . . ." [p. 432]). The third kind is thus reserved for the extreme creativity only found in men of genius: ". . . those who attain it utter—without study or guidance—things so delicate, so true and prodigious, that they have never occurred to men before, or been seen, heard, or written down" (p. 433).

In the new edition, Huarte also develops the notion of certain kinds of "inabilities" to be found in man, which bear some correlation with man's positive intellectual capacities, as he has described them. A certain class of men are so lacking in creativity, claims Huarte, that they may be said to be intellectually "castrated." They are unteachable and "differ very little from the brute beasts" (p. 437). A second group includes those men who are to a certain extent able to respond positively, but who are still somewhat limited: "They are like some women who become pregnant and give birth, but whose children die as they are born" (p. 438). A third kind of inability is found in those men of letters who are creative but who lack discipline and organization, and therefore become confused (". . . like the woman who becomes pregnant and gives birth to a child with its head where its feet should be, and eyes in the back of its head" [p. 438]). A fourth kind of inability is illustrated by those who learn something well off by heart, but who, when prompted and questioned on aspects of what they have learnt, reveal a basically imperfect and partial grasp of the material. Such people speak by instinct, like brutes, and their words carry far more meaning than they themselves realize. They are in fact close to being automata (pp. 438–39).

In addition to the above quantitative analysis of man in terms of his three wits, Huarte also believed that man can be categorized qualitatively, in terms of whether his memory, understanding, or imagination is dominant. This was to provide the basis for his categorization of the sciences, insofar as he believed that each discipline favors a particular faculty. It is difficult to say to what extent there is a correlation between the quantitative and qualitative analyses. Huarte recognizes that in practice most disciplines favor a combination of faculties, one of which is dominant, and it seems clear that each wit is made up of a similar combination. The first wit is certainly strongly associated with the memory, but Huarte is vague and ambiguous about the respective roles of the understanding and imagination as they function with regard to the second and third wits. This ambiguity stems from a deep-seated ambivalence toward the imagination. Although he sees the understanding as a creative force, indeed, as *the* creative faculty (p. 427 ff.), there are clear indications that Huarte felt the need to temper his rationalism. Hence, despite his general distrust of the imagination, he seems to have suspected at times that this faculty played a crucial role in at least some intellectual activity of a creative kind. In an off-guarded moment he looks to the imagination as the source of the intellectual turmoil that stimulated him to undertake his investigation, the results of which are contained in the *Examen* (p. 418). Indeed, he is inclined to associate the third, creative wit with poetic inspiration (pp. 433–34), and poetry, we recall, is categorized by him under the imagination (p. 164). Moreover, in the discussion of medicine, the validity of intuition as a means of knowing is explicitly recognized. Emphasizing the importance of practical knowledge in the actual curing of patients, Huarte writes: "In order to attain this knowledge, the imagination has certain inexplicable properties by which it is able to ascertain things in ways impossible to describe or understand. Nor does there exist any body of rules by which to master these ways" (p. 234). The doctor himself is no more able to explain the workings of these hidden processes than is the scientist. Suffice to say that they are highly complex (the imagination works with signs which are "familiar, uncertain, conjectural, and constantly shifting"), rapid ("in a twinkling of the eye"), and reliable.

Huarte's ideas on creativity have been seen as anticipating seventeenth-century speculation.[4] Whatever the validity of this view, it is important to realize that Huarte was also continuing a medieval precedent. Thomas Aquinas followed the Aristotelian doctrine of the mind as a *tabula rasa*, but made some concessions to the Platonic view, thereby steering a mid-course between the two extremes. Thomistic Scholastics believed that the mind is not simply a reflection of external reality, but that knowledge is a product of two factors: the object that is perceived and the mind that does the perceiving. The mind possesses a creative force, the *intellectus agens*, which operates upon sense data. The obtaining of knowledge thus has both a passive aspect and an active one.[5]

Nevertheless, despite his possible indebtedness to the medieval Thomistic tradition, Huarte certainly infused the doctrine of creativity with a new lease of life, and transposed it into a different context, namely, that of the Renaissance exaltation of the dignity of man. For Renaissance scholars such as Huarte, man's excellence was conditional upon his freedom, by which he became God-like. Made by God in an image less than perfect, man yet possessed the capacity to improve, to become more like the original, and it was this striving for the infinite that was the sign of his divine origin. The creative instinct had its field of operation in culture, which, as a world of becoming, contrasted sharply with the static world of nature. In this context, Renaissance scholars rejuvenated and reinterpreted the myth of Prometheus, which so effectively reflected their vision of man as a creature born imperfect but capable of a second creation. Increasingly, they cast man in the role of a Promethean creator, the rival rather than the slave of creative nature.[6] Huarte embodies supremely this self-affirmation of the ego. Other Renaissance scholars expressed their opposition to astrology, and some did so on the grounds that this pseudoscience limited man's freedom to an unacceptable degree. But few spoke with a greater conviction than Huarte when he succinctly dismissed astrology as an irredeemably arbitrary (and therefore misguided) system which precluded human control of natural events (p. 343). The fact was that the author of the *Examen* had no patience with anything that suggested a passive, not to say cowardly, acceptance of the superficial and chaotic. With the power of his intellect and with this alone he would grasp the design of what lies beyond, and discover truth.

Man is creative not only in culture, but also in society. The Renaissance developed the ideal of the self-made man—an ideal which Huarte passionately shared. In a country where "purity of blood" rather than outstanding individual initiative and behavior was generally seen as the necessary qualification for membership of the aristocracy, Huarte took the daring step of basing his concept of nobility (*hidalguía*) on the recognition of feats of bravery and daring. After reminding us that in chess a pawn can become a queen, he suggests a parallel with social advancement: "Because all the fine noble families that there have been and will be in the world have originated, and will originate, in nobodies and ordinary individuals who courageously performed such deeds that they won for themselves and their descendants the title of *hidalgos*, knights, nobles, counts, marquises, dukes, and kings" (p. 272). Huarte rejects the idea that nobility is eternal. In his view the only innate nobility is that which each man possesses as a birthright, whatever his station in life. It is true, he concedes, that titles can be inherited, but it should be clear that they are all ultimately the gift of the king. In short, the author of the *Examen* seeks to equate inherited nobility ("hidalguía de sangre") with that received directly from the monarch in living memory ("hidalguía de privilegio"). To illustrate these points, he tells of a certain encounter between a captain and a knight. When the latter showed condescension to the former by the subtle use of forms of address, the captain retaliated with a lecture on nobility and honor, both of which he saw, rightly in Huarte's view, as the rewards of personal valor. Few Renaissance scholars, it seems, were as sensitive to the anomalies of birth as the humble physician from San Juan.

Though Huarte exalted man's unique status in creation, he was also a powerful influence in the opposite direction. As we have seen, he developed a theory of man's nature that effectively negated the claim that man was distinguished above all by his freedom. In the context of his doctrine of rigorous determinism, Huarte showed this freedom to be, if not illusory, at least of a severely circumscribed kind. His work begins with two truisms: firstly, that unless a child is naturally gifted, his study and labor to attain an art will avail him nothing; secondly, that children obviously vary in natural ability. His central obsession was to explain why, despite the undisputed equality of their faculties of the soul, men differed in performance, an undeniable fact supported by authorities and his own personal experience. Huarte attempts an initial clarification by asking what is meant by the word *nature*. He believed a definition of this key term was essential. (He was always sufficiently distrustful of language to avoid being deceived by words.) He felt that *nature* was not an irreducible concept, but a bucket term into which we pour all that we do not

understand about men. He himself defines the term thus:
". . . the temperament formed by the four primary qualities
(heat, cold, humidity, and dryness) is what will be called
nature . . ." (p. 87).

Climate, food, age, and sex affect men via the four qualities,
which affect the body, which in turn influences the soul. As
regards climate and food, we have already seen Huarte explain
Jewish expertise in medicine in these terms. Climate as a condi-
tioning factor of human behavior was one of his fundamental
preoccupations. For example, concerning the problem of why the
northern countries of Europe exhibit such skill in language-
learning, he writes: ". . . those who live in the north are lacking
in understanding, and those who live between the septentrion
and the torrid zone are very prudent. Prudence is a quality most
relevant to our own region, a fact it is impossible to deny if we
consider that Spain is neither as cold as the northern lands, nor as
hot as the torrid zone" (p. 175). Similarly, Huarte was always
convinced that man's intellectual development was closely dependent upon the natural rhythm of his life cycle: "In man's second
age, which is adolescence, he should work on the art of ratiocination, because it is then that the understanding
develops . . . When youth arrives, all the other sciences governed
by the understanding can be learned . . ." (pp. 74–75). As
regards sex, we will see later that Huarte found here one of the
most decisive factors in the formation of human character.

Huarte held that the seat of the intelligence was in the head. In
chapters III and IV of the *Examen*, he explains how the brain
consists of four ventricles, in which are lodged the three faculties
of the mind, these being the imagination, memory, and
understanding. According to Huarte, the brain needs certain
qualities if the rational soul is to function properly. It must have
first of all a "good composition," which consists of a correct form,
sufficient quantity, and a good arrangement of average-sized
ventricles. Regarding the form, Huarte echoes Galen: ". . . it
should be just as if one had taken a perfectly round ball of wax
and pressed it lightly on both sides. In this way the forehead and
back of the head bulge slightly. From which it follows that, if a
man has a very flat forehead and his head is straight at the back,
he does not have the proportions necessary for intelligence and
ability" (pp. 91–92). As regards the size of the brain, quantity is
obviously a condition of intelligence, which explains why man

has the largest brain and why the most intelligent animals resemble him in this respect. However, the bulk should not consist of flesh and bone: "What I have discovered from experience is that, in the cases of men with small bodies, it is better for the head to be on the large side, and in the cases of more heavily built men, on the small; and the reason is that in this way one achieves the moderate quantity appropriate for the functioning of the rational soul" (p. 93). Finally, the ventricles are to be well arranged, with one in a central position, two on either side, and one at the back.

Another feature of the brain required by the rational soul is that its different parts function very much as a unit. This natural coordination is often lost as a result of injuries to the head, which cause some men to lose their memory, others their understanding, and others their imagination (p. 94). To conclude, Huarte suggests that the brain should possess only a moderate heat with no excess of other qualities; and should have "delicate and subtle substance and composition in its parts" (p. 94).

A difficult problem to explain was how the *three* faculties relate to the *four* ventricles of the brain. It was generally accepted by scholars that the job of the ventricles was to turn the *vital* into the *animal spirits*. Huarte agreed with Galen that the central ventricle alone served this function. This seemed to leave the other three ventricles to correspond with the three faculties. However, Huarte argued that, since each faculty needs each ventricle, there can exist no one-to-one match. As to why there should be *three* ventricles, he merely suggested that it was for the same reason we have two eyes and two ears, namely, the more the merrier (pp. 119–20).

What is beyond dispute is that the three faculties are causally related to three of the elements (cold being excluded as serving only to moderate heat). The understanding favors dryness, the memory moisture, and the imagination heat. In this way Huarte argues that men can be categorized into "memoriosos," "imaginativos," and "intelectivos," though he insists there are many subdivisions (p. 129). Sudden changes of temperament affect the functioning of the three faculties, which are closely bound up with certain of man's arts and sciences. Hence, a sudden change that favors the memory may lead a man to show suddenly unbelievable linguistic skills. Cases of insanity are also explained in the same way, as a result, that is, of radical imbalance in the temperament. Since he realizes that in practice the three faculties intermingle in their work, Huarte naturally concludes that no discipline can be said to be dominated *entirely* by one faculty. He uses the same theoretical framework to account for animal instinct: "And among animals of the same species, the most easily trained and intelligent is the one with the most temperate brain; and if, for some reason, such as an illness, the delicate temperament of the brain is disturbed, the animal will then lose its prudence and ability, in the same way as a man" (p. 104).

In this way, nature chains man within his category, and, by the changes of his temperament, he is imprisoned deterministically in a rigid process of cause and effect, from which he can hardly escape to exercise his free will. Any freedom he has lies in his understanding and control of his own temperament. The body dominates the soul, and man's status in the Chain of Being is thus brought into question. Free will is an illusion and so too is creativity, being dependent, like insanity, on sudden changes of temperament. In the context of Huarte's rationalistic science, "creativity" and "freedom" were extraneous, mysterious elements which needed to be explained away.

Not surprisingly, Huarte came to embrace a view of man that is essentially pessimistic, insofar as he believed the very temper of man's body inclines him to vice: "For it is impossible to create a man who is perfect in all his powers, no matter how temperate his body may be; impossible to prevent the irascible and concupiscent faculties from controlling reason and inciting man to sin. Thus, it is not wise to allow any man, however temperate, to follow his natural inclination, without restraining him and correcting him in accordance with reason" (p. 294). If a man is to function properly physically, he must possess considerable heat in the heart, with which the liver is able to digest food and produce blood, but this very heat is a source of disturbance to the brain. Moreover, Huarte continues, "man's will, being free, reacts, and becomes inclined to surrender to his baser instincts. This clearly shows that nature cannot create a man who is perfect in all his powers and yet inclined to virtue" (pp. 295–96).

Theologically speaking, Huarte was naturally inclined to emphasize man's fallen state, though his doctrine of original sin was, to say the least, idiosyncratic. Adam was the most perfect man ever created (with the exception of Christ), but, had not God infused in him a supernatural quality with which to control his baser instincts, he would have readily surrendered to sin:

"Because the irascible and concupiscent faculties are so powerful on account of the heat, and the rational faculty so weak and unable to oppose them, God furnished man with a supernatural quality which the theologians call *natural justice*, with which to repress the baser instincts; and man's reason thereby remained superior, and man was inclined to virtue. But when our first parents sinned, this quality was lost, whereas the irascible and concupiscent faculties retained their former strength and were therefore superior to reason . . ." (p. 297). This view has more in common with Augustinianism, and ultimately with Lutheranism, than with strict Catholic doctrine, which has never taught that man is in need of supernatural aid in order to act in accordance with Natural Law. However, this brings us on to the subjects of reason and faith and the doctrine of free will, which will be discussed in the following chapters.

In conclusion, Huarte's exaltation of the dignity of man, particularly with respect to his ability to control his own destiny, suggests a personal commitment to a philosophy of liberalism. The extent of his commitment, however, is deceptive, for the author of the *Examen* gradually emerges as a scholar who, in an attempt to extend the realms of science, undercut many key terms in the vocabulary of liberalism. Indeed, his ultimate goal seems to have been nothing less than the exorcism of the "ghost in the machine," and, in order to achieve this, he believed that it was necessary for the scientist to carry investigation into a realm beyond freedom and dignity.

CHAPTER 6

Reason versus Faith

I   *The Doctrine of Double-Truth*

ONE of the major achievements of medieval philosophy be-tween the ninth century, when scholarship emerged from the darkness caused by the collapse of Rome, and the thirteenth cen-tury was the establishment of harmony between Faith and Reason. The task was not an easy one. On one side lay those who would trivialize the Scriptures in dry philosophical analysis, and, on the other, those who would defend at all cost the profound mysteries of the faith. Between these two extremes Thomas Aquinas erected a philosophy based on a reconciliation of faith and reason, seeing both as ultimately derived from God. Within Thomism, each has its respective, autonomous sphere, for it is deemed that reason considers things in themselves, according to their proper causes, whereas theology is concerned with the First Cause, which is God. Reason should be allowed to pursue its own goals unimpeded, provided, of course, that it does not transgress its bounds; whereas faith should deal with those kinds of knowledge of the Divine that lie beyond the ken of reason. Yet for Thomists the relationship between the two realms is more com-plex than might seem to be the case at first. They judge that reason depends upon faith for a direction, for an indication of the ends it might attain; whereas faith, even less independent than reason, is always bound to refer to its partner, upon whom it relies to be made credible. Despite such interaction, however, both reason and faith remain spheres with their own inalienable identities.[1]

Fourteenth-century nominalists such as Ockham were the first to challenge the Thomistic synthesis.[2] By establishing a void be-tween theology and philosophy, these Nominalists prepared the ground for the more radical attempts by certain Renaissance scholars to base theological doctrine exclusively on faith and the sciences on reason, and thereby develop a rigorously defined doctrine of double-truth. The most famous exponent of this doctrine is Pomponazzi, who, in a famous essay (1516) on the immortality of the soul, argued that such immortality must be accepted as an article of faith, and that it cannot be demonstrated on rational grounds. This dualism of faith and reason has been widely discussed by modern scholars, who, according to their own beliefs, have interpreted the work of such writers as Pomponazzi either as atheism, thinly veiled to avoid the watchful eyes of the Inquisition, or as Catholicism, similarly disguised to pander to the secularism of the age. Kristeller, however, has questioned the validity of both these views, suggesting that Pomponazzi's essay is based on a genuine dilemma, involving a conflict between the equally appealing and persuasive, if at times contradictory, claims of faith and reason.[3] We have seen that Huartean scholarship has followed much the same pattern as that relating to Pomponazzi, presenting us with conflicting interpretations of Huarte as a sincere and devout Catholic, as an unbeliever, and, I suggest, the most realistic one, of Huarte as a scholar with sincerely divided views.

There can be no doubt Huarte himself was committed to a purely rationalistic interpretation of reality, despite his awareness of the uncertainty of reason. He stubbornly maintained that miraculous explanations were, in science, illegitimate, short-cut solutions, and that it was possible to explain human nature in rationalist terms. The view often expressed by the common people that it is God who makes men able or otherwise is true, but not a correct "manner of speaking." God is certainly the *universal* cause of all that happens in the universe, but the scientist is interested, or should be, in secondary causes, on the basis of which causal networks can be explained. Only by restricting his gaze in this way can the scientist reveal the order and patterning that God built into nature when He created it. The laws of nature are, for Huarte, comparable to those of a monarch. Both types of law prevail in normal circumstances within their respective spheres, and are only abrogated briefly in exceptional cases, as when God performs a miracle or (continuing the parallel) the king grants a pardon. Too much reliance on direct divine intervention as an explanation of natural phenomena threatens the work of the scientist by enlarging the

sphere of the arbitrary, and therefore of the chaotic and un-
predictable, which is anathema to systematic, rational inquiry
(pp. 80–85). Hence Huarte's forceful criticism of Plato's view of
the creative wit as god-given: ". . . and it is unbecoming in such
a major philosopher as Plato that he should have recourse to
universal causes, without first seeking the particular ones with
great diligence and care" (p. 433). Similarly, he objects to Galen's
irrational appeals to divine agency when trying to explain "instinct": "But this is a manner of speaking which we have
previously criticized, because it is not fitting that natural
philosophers should reduce effects immediately to God, leaving
aside the intermediary causes" (p. 100). To illustrate in some
detail his objections to unscientific procedure, Huarte tells the
story of a debate between a grammarian and a natural
philosopher. Both were asked by a gardener why the plants he set
did not respond to his constant digging, raking, watering, and
manuring, whereas the weeds flourished. Huarte writes: "The
grammarian replied that such an effect was attributable to divine
Providence. . . . This was a reply that greatly amused the
natural philosopher, who saw appeal was being made to God
through ignorance both of the workings of natural causes and of
the way in which these produce their effects" (p. 81). Huarte
naturally agreed with the criticism directed against the grammarian. This was not a question to be dealt with by the
metaphysician or theologian, and hence the appeal to Providence
was out of place: ". . . the question posed by the gardener is
natural, and falls under the jurisdiction of natural philosophers,
because there are observable, sequential causes from which such
an effect [i.e., the behavior of the plants and weeds] can be born"
(p. 81). The age of miracles is over, and the recourse to them by
way of explanation of events is an "antiquated manner of
speaking."

A question that immediately suggested itself to Huarte—as
always fascinated by the psychology of human behavior—was
why people should be so disposed to use miracles as an explanation of phenomena. Firstly, he argues, they are impatient, for the
task of scientific explanation is arduous, whereas the miraculous
solution is quick and easy; secondly, supernatural influence gives
them a sense of importance, of being singled out for God's special
attention; and thirdly, miracles are held to enhance the glory of
God, whom people look upon as a worker of wonderful deeds.

Huarte had little sympathy with laziness and facile explanation, or with excessively anthropocentric views of the universe; and he clearly believed it cheapened God to see him as a master magician (pp. 83–84). He realized, moreover, that the appeal to the First Cause posed insuperable theological and moral problems, for when things go wrong in nature, as when a child is born deformed, the tendency to attribute all to God runs the risk of heresy: ". . . one must not praise nature for such works or consider her wise. And if God were the author, He would not be able to prevent any of these imperfections [in man]. According to Plato, only the first men in the world were made by God, the rest being born through the operation of secondary causes . . ." (p. 101). He thus remained adamant in his initial standpoint, maintaining that the sign of aptitude for natural philosophy in a student is the refusal to "attribute everything to the miraculous" (p. 84).

This purely rational approach, however, had the drawback already discussed: the lack of a touchstone by which to evaluate theories. We have seen how at times Huarte appeared to embrace a skeptical standpoint which admitted all judgments as equally valid, but also how he refused to resign himself to such defeatism, and succeeded in extricating himself from the mire of doubt which threatened to engulf him. Relativism had, for Huarte, no place within the realm of science as such, and the eclecticism of the Humanists proved much too superficial for his purposes. Hence he attacked the orator's skepticism and his irresponsible lack of rigor and commitment in the quest for truth. Though himself eclectic to the extent that he drew upon many sources, he did not believe in defending irresponsibly any given standpoint with the power of rhetoric, after the manner of the Sophists and Humanists. His own borrowings were made with strict reference to the theoretical framework he intended to establish in the *Examen*.

Yet in committing himself so totally to rationalism, Huarte set himself, inadvertently and unwittingly, one suspects, on a collision course with the Inquisition. The major confrontation took place over the question of the immortality of the soul. We witnessed with respect to Thomistic philosophy that, though a division between the realms of faith and reason is easily drawn in theory, in practice the dividing line is blurred. For a man of science there is always the temptation in this situation to extend illegitimately (in orthodox terms) the bounds of reason. Hence, though Huarte's faith led him to support the Platonic belief in the immortality and incorporeality of the soul—he describes it as being "illustrious" and "Catholic" (p. 151)—, his own rationalistic materialism was more consonant with the Galenic view of the soul as inextricably bound up with the corrupt body. The solution could only be that of double-truth: "And thus it is a fact that the infallible certainty of our souls being immortal is not based on rational argument; even less are there reasons to prove our soul is corruptible. Arguments both for and against can be easily refuted: only our divine faith makes us certain and convinced that our soul will live eternally" (p. 152). These are the words, it seems to me, not of a heretic disguising his orthodoxy, nor of a Catholic merely making concessions to reason, but of a man in a genuine dilemma. Huarte's use of the doctrine of double-truth, however, does not seem calculated: he appeals to it as a man who has unwittingly argued himself into a tight corner. Having launched himself on his rational inquiry and found himself, unexpectedly, in a position untenable in terms of Christian dogma, he was obliged to backpedal furiously.

When Huarte's doctrine of double-truth began to show signs of strain and even to crumble visibly, it was inevitable, given his commitment to a scientific procedure, that reason should encroach upon faith. This is shown by his tendency to treat the Bible as a scientific text, to be elucidated in rationalist terms. He speculates as to how, if his theory of somatic influences on the soul is correct, souls separated from the body can continue to function (pp. 158–60); and suggests Christ can be classified with respect to the psychological categories established in the *Examen* (pp. 305–06). Huarte's whole approach here not only ill becomes a person such as himself, so confessedly concerned to abide by scientific methodology, but above all shows in its crude literalism a complete insensitivity to the mysteries and spiritual values of Christianity and its texts.

The traffic was certainly not all one-way. By the same bridge, the supernatural and superstitious passed into the heart of science. Since he objected to any appeal to God as a direct agent in causation, one would have expected Huarte to oppose for the same reasons any reference to the Devil. It comes as no surprise, therefore, to find him objecting to the common explanation of fits in the following manner: "[Second-rate philosophers], on seeing themselves surrounded by the subtle and delicate phenomena [which are the concern] of natural philosophy, would have the ignorant believe that God or the Devil are the authors of strange, prodigious effects, whose natural causes they neither know of nor understand" (pp. 112–13). Nevertheless, Satan and his works figure prominently in the *Examen*, for example, when Huarte compares the capabilities of the rational soul to those of devils (p. 114). Though the modern reader may be inclined to see such discussion as irrational nonsense and an unfortunate aberration in an otherwise sensible writer, illustrating Huarte's failure to operate a doctrine of double-truth in the rigorous manner he himself demanded, it is important to recall that the supernatural played a not insignificant role in the early Scientific Revolution. Historians of science now acknowledge the extent to which the revolutionary progress made by such scholars as Paracelsus, Copernicus, and Bruno was motivated by a deep conviction of the working of occult forces beyond the range of immediate observation.[4] When they undertook to weed their gardens of superstitious nonsense, Huarte and his fellow scientists did not find it easy to recognize the undesirable plants.

Despite such inconsistencies, however, there can be no doubt as to the direction that the *Examen* took. The Renaissance witnessed a shift from the religio-philosophical view of the world to a natural-philosophical view which was based on the empirical investigation of natural causes, and Huarte played a major role in furthering the transition. He shared closely in the attempt to put theology politely but firmly in its place, so that science could pursue its own goals unshackled by "matters of faith and morals." Without the groundwork carried out by such scholars as Huarte, the rapid advances of the seventeenth century might have been much retarded, if not rendered impossible.

II *The Immortality of the Soul*

Huarte's commitment to rationalism was not inherently in conflict with established theological opinion. As regards the concept of fortune, for example, it led him to conclusions remarkably consonant with Christian belief. The concept of fortune, though it had continued to capture the popular imagination from classical times, had often been condemned by Christian thinkers as incompatible with the notion of an omnipotent god. Huarte also believed, though for different reasons, that fortune, carefully considered, turns out to be one of those concepts that can be explained away. There is, he insisted, a more rational way of explaining human behavior and historical causation, and "[b]ecause natural philosophers did not hit upon it, they invented such a foolish and nonsensical cause as is that of Fortune, to which they could attribute good and bad happenings, as opposed to the imprudence or wisdom of men" (p. 268).

In other respects Huarte's rational procedure led to conclusions somewhat less compatible with established theological doctrine. We have suggested this was particularly true of his treatment of the question of the immortality of man's soul, a topic around which the doctrine of double-truth took shape in the Renaissance. His views on the subject are worth considering more closely in their traditional context.

The doctrine of immortality was not only adumbrated in the popular and religious thought of the ancient world but was also discussed explicitly by Greek philosophers. Scholarly treatment varied. Plato and his followers supported the doctrine decisively, whereas Aristotle was rather ambiguous. Not surprisingly, given the continuing influence of these two philosophers, the treatment of the subject in the Christian tradition has been uncertain. As Kristeller writes:

It is clear that some notions of a future life appear in the Old Testament and that the New Testament speaks very explicitly about the kingdom of God, eternal life, and resurrection. It is also true that body and soul are repeatedly distinguished in the New Testament and that at least one passage speaks of the future life of the soul [EV. Matt. 10:28]. However, the writers of the Bible were no professional philosophers and had a very slight, if any, acquaintance with Greek philosophy and its terminology. There is an occasional, but not a consistent distinction between body and soul and no hard and fast statement that the soul (or even God) is incorporeal, or that the soul is immortal, let alone by nature. The majority of recent theologians have been led to admit that there is no scriptural basis for the natural immortality of the soul. . .[5]

Though the doctrine of the immortality and incorporeality of the soul figured prominently in St. Augustine, who drew upon Plato and the Neoplatonists, it ceased to be of central concern with the rise of Scholasticism in the late Middle Ages and the establishment of Aristotle as *the* authority. When it did figure in discussion, a skeptical note is sometimes in evidence. Duns Scotus, for example, found traditional arguments for immortality singularly inconclusive, while the Averroists' teaching on the unity of the intellect offered an even greater threat. Kristeller concludes: ". . . we arrive at the curious and unexpected conclusion that the doctrine of immortalilty did not play a major role in medieval thought, especially not during the thirteenth and fourteenth centuries when the teachings of Aristotle and his commentators tended to prevail. The central importance which the doctrine came to assume during the Renaissance thus appears in a new perspective . . ."[6]

The "this-worldly" outlook of the Renaissance (in contrast to the "other-worldliness" of the Middle Ages), together with the increasing concern with the individual and with personal experience, doubtless explains, at least in part, why the subject of man's personal survival in an after-life assumed a special importance in this age. For some scholars, the very dignity of man and his eminence in the scheme of things rested on his possession of an immortal soul. A major landmark in the discussion was Pomponazzi's famous essay on the subject of the immortality of the soul. The Aristotelian philosopher argued at some length that immortality cannot be demonstrated on natural, rational grounds, but must be accepted as an article of faith. His treatise aroused considerable opposition, though it provoked no response from the Inquisition. It is important to note, in view of Huarte's own treatment of the subject, that the dependence of the soul on the body figured prominently in Pomponazzi's arguments against immortality.

This was the historical setting to Huarte's study of the nature of the soul and the organic relationship between the brain and the understanding. He realized the complexity and dangers involved in discussing the subject, but his intellectual integrity compelled him to deal with it, central as it was to any discussion of man's identity. He begins by considering the faculties of the soul as organic: ". . . we have turned the understanding (along with the imagination and memory) into an organic faculty . . ." (p. 134). Huarte presents this view in explicit opposition to Aristotle and his followers, whom he interprets as believing that the soul was an entity free of the body. He realizes that, whereas the argument for immortality follows naturally from the Aristotelian standpoint, his own position raises serious problems. His discussion,

however, is uncertain in its direction. He certainly finds
Aristotle's proofs of the soul's inorganicity "so efficacious" as to appear to defy refutation: ". . . to this faculty [i.e., the understand-
ing] belongs the task of discovering and understanding the nature
and composition of all the material objects there are in the world;
and if it were itself joined to any corporeal object, this in itself
would prevent its discovering all other such objects. We can see
this as regards the five senses, for if one's sense of taste is bitter,
everything the tongue comes into contact with tastes bitter; and if
the crystalline humor is green or yellow, everything the eye sees is
judged to be the same color" (p. 135). Aristotle found repugnant
the idea that the understanding should be affected by
temperature.

However, Huarte was not persuaded by such arguments:

The reasons on which Aristotle bases his views are of little moment, for it
does not follow that, because the understanding must deal with material
things, it can have no corporeal organ. The corporeal qualities which are
part of the actual makeup of an organ do not affect the faculty. . . . This
can be seen clearly with respect to touch, for, although the hand consists
of four material qualities and possesses itself quantity and softness or hard-
ness, it is still able to judge whether a thing is hot or cold, hard or soft, or
whether it is large or small. If we are asked why the natural heat of the
hand does not prevent our touch from sensing the heat of the stove, we
reply that the qualities involved in the makeup of the organ do not affect
the organ itself, nor do they influence how it functions in any way.
Similarly, it is through the eye that we learn of the shape and size of
things, and it is also apparent that the eye itself has its own dimensions of
shape and size, and consists of humors and tunicles, some of which are col-
ored, and some clear and transparent. But we are not prevented thereby
from using our vision to discover the shape and size of objects which are
placed before us. (pp. 139–40)

Huarte was able, of course, to find evidence of contradiction in
Aristotle himself, whose teachings on the nature of the soul, as
suggested above, were somewhat ambiguous. Huarte insists:
"If the understanding were separate from the body and dissociated from heat, cold, humidity, and dryness, and from the
other corporeal qualities, it would follow that all men would
reason equally well. And experience tells us that some men can
understand and reason better than others" (p. 138). Huarte is
aware that the Aristotelians oppose this argument by claiming
that differences in ability derive from the relative malfunctioning

of the imagination and memory, upon which the understanding is dependent for the furnishing of images. As he also notes, however, they thereby contradict Aristotle's theory regarding the independence of the faculties.

Having shown such hesitancy when discussing the question of the soul's substance, Huarte was bound to treat the subject of its immortality in an equally indecisive manner. Plato's view that "the rational soul was an incorporeal, spiritual substance, not subject to corruption or to mortality . . ." (p. 151) must have convinced him that there existed a correlation between the arguments for inorganicity and for immortality, and he obviously realized that the belief in the soul's spirituality was orthodox, Catholic doctrine. Nevertheless, his argument develops in a curiously halting manner. He reminds us, significantly one feels, that Galen, on seeing a sane man become delirious through an overheated brain, rejected the Platonic view (p. 151), and implies that the onus of explaining such apparent influence of the body on the soul lies with Plato. At the same time, he seems to have little sympathy with Galen, who, on failing to find a Platonist able to resolve his doubts, refused to abandon his own standpoint. Huarte supposes that the Greek physician could only have learned of his error at his death.

It is hard to decide how to interpret Huarte's words here, to capture, that is, their exact tone and reveal unambiguously what is his view. One senses that he realizes that just as the theory of the inorganicity of the soul was seen to correspond to that of immortality, so his own view of the soul's organicity pointed toward the mortality of the soul. His detailed recording of Galen's unanswered objection to Plato's views suggests some sympathy for the physician's doubts. However, he saw that Galen's was not the orthodox Christian view, and, pointing to the basis of this view in faith as opposed to reason, he spiritedly continues to criticize the Greek doctor for his "deceitful arguments." The imperfections of the body should not be attributed to the soul, Huarte argues, just as those of the universe should not be attributed to its Creator. As if sensing his analysis was becoming ragged and meandering, Huarte suddenly concludes: "Galen's error lies in wishing to verify by the principles of natural philosophy whether the soul, deprived of the body, dies or not, this being a question which is properly treated by a superior science and one with firmer principles . . ." (p. 154). By these principles, Huarte proclaims, we can know that the soul of man is not corruptible. The doctrine of double-truth was never used to greater effect.

Huarte's ensuing discussion regarding the claims of faith and reason inevitably becomes somewhat inconsistent and contradictory, as the author of the *Examen* bewilderingly views the question now from one position, now from another. He argues that spirits, such as the Devil, are affected by material forces, without impairment to their spirituality, but immediately concedes that no natural philosopher would accept this argument, for he will fail to see how the rational soul, being spiritual, could be altered by heat, cold, humidity, and dryness: "These difficulties and arguments were rather embarrassing for Galen and for present-day philosophers . . ." (p. 158). Huarte himself assures us that he does not share these doubts, and argues with Aristotle to the effect that, just as a substance is subject to its accidents, so the accidents of the body "affect the substance, which is the rational soul . . ." (p. 158). It goes without saying, of course, that the soul also influenced the body. There follows in the *Examen* an extensive section of biblical exegesis to prove that the Devil and the rational soul can use the senses without the aid of a material body.

In the revised edition of his work Huarte was obliged to have second thoughts on the subject of the soul. Having in 1575 tied each faculty of the mind to a corresponding physical organ (p. 117), he was obliged to confess in 1594 that "for the understanding, nature made no such instrument . . ." (p. 385). A careful consideration of the new material in the *Examen*, however, reveals that Huarte's basic position remained the same as before, albeit somewhat disguised. In the added sections and emendations, he continues to insist that the understanding does work with images ("fantasmas") furnished by the other faculties (p. 385), and that, despite equality of understanding in men, individuals do hold different opinions regarding specific problems (pp. 418–19). He explains that "because the understanding depends on the other faculties in order to perform its role and these depend on the brain as an organ in order to function, we say that the human brain must have the conditions that we have outlined in order that the rational soul can function with it in a manner appropriate to the species" (p. 385).

The above comments prepared the ground for a more detailed discussion in an extensive addition in the new edition of 1594. In a completely new chapter, Huarte notes how Galen, when considering the effect on the body of such phenomena as climate, deduced that "all the habits and abilities of the rational soul accord without exception with the temperament of the body in which it is" (p. 440). Hence the Greek doctor reprehends moral philosophers for not seeing that medicine has a moral dimension, claiming that foods and drugs directly influence vices and virtues. In contrast, Christian dogma, Huarte accepts, sees virtues as exclusively *spiritual* habits, contained within the rational soul, and presents the soul as the mover of the body, which is the passive partner. He elucidates: "And if virtues and vices were habits that depended on the temperament, it would follow that man would function as a natural rather than free agent . . ." (p. 440). Here he isolates for consideration the central issue at stake, namely, that of free will. To accept that the soul is conditioned by the body is to deny free will, or so Huarte would seem to be arguing. Yet we have seen that Huarte's own natural philosophy pointed in this direction. Hence, though apparently maintaining that the soul is not governed by the body, he is understandably impressed by the fact that Aristotle, Plato, Hippocrates, and Galen all believed that the latter does influence the former. Huarte thus appears finally to commit a *volte face*: ". . . it should be apparent that *perfect* virtues, as they are conceived by moral philosophers, are spiritual habits tied to the rational soul, whose being does not depend on the temperature of the body. But having said that, it is true that there is no virtue or vice in man . . . which does not have its own temperature in the members of the body . . ." (p. 441). Though Huarte is careful to insist that one can always overcome one's temperament, and thus maintain freedom of will, he yet notes that this is only possible "with great strife and conflict" (p. 441).

In short, we should not look in the *Examen* for any exalted view of man's inner battle, in which the forces of Good engage those of Evil. Huarte believes it would be more expedient to eradicate any conflict by the judicious use of medicine and other measures to manipulate the temperament. It is clear that he was unwilling to abandon his 1575 view of man as a creature ultimately dependent upon God's grace: ". . . if a man is to perform some virtuous act against the inclinations of the flesh, it is impossible to do so without the exterior help of grace, because the qualities with which the lower faculty works are of greater efficacy. . . . Hence, without the Catholic Church's needing to teach us, natural philosophy tells us that we cannot conquer our nature unless we receive special help from God. And the fact is that grace strengthens our will" (pp. 297–98).

We know that Huarte embraced a doctrine of double-truth, which attempted to delimit clearly the areas of activity of faith and reason. In practice, however, it proved impossible to maintain an absolute division, particularly when attempting to discuss rationally a subject that, in its very nature, seems closely tied to the spiritual side of man, namely, the question of the immortality of the soul. Huarte's work is an admirable illustration of the inherent instability of a dualist view of man's nature, and the difficulty experienced by its exponents in not emphasizing one side of the dualism to the exclusion of the other. Huarte felt ultimately little certainty about anything, but he undoubtedly found the material world more reassuring than the spiritual. He observed that the spatio-temporal world, including within it man's body, obeys a unified set of laws, and he tried to extend these to hidden regions of man's being. Though accepting that the mind exists apart from other phenomena, Huarte argued in such a way that, within the context of his ideas, the realm of the spirit came to form an increasingly smaller part of the totality of things. He believed physical principles had proved their efficacy in yielding solutions to many problems, and merely tried to extend their domain. In an interactionist, such as himself, who believed that physical events occurring in the brain are causally and immediately related to spiritual events, the extension was not difficult. Finally, therefore, the doctrine of double-truth went by the board, and Huarte came into conflict with religion.

CHAPTER 7

Pedagogical Theory and Practice

I *Tradition and Reform*

TRADITIONAL education in the sixteenth century, though by no means devoid of speculative excitement and controversy, both of which were sometimes found in abundance in universities, was yet undeniably characterized by methods antagonistic to intellectual curiosity. Huarte was very familiar with its deficiencies. He himself no doubt passed through all the normal stages of education, which were relatively uniform in Europe. He would have had to follow the traditional trivium, consisting of grammar, dialectic, and rhetoric, and the quadrivium, made up of arithmetic, geometry, astronomy, and the theory of music. This would have provided him and his fellow students with a fairly broad basis, before some of them continued to more specialized work in medicine, theology, and canon or civil law, which were the disciplines of higher degrees. The uniformity of education found at the first degree stage did not exist to the same extent at a higher level, separate institutions often developing a reputation for excellence in a particular field. Alcalá, for example, was particularly famous for its medical school, which attracted such students as Huarte from far and wide.

Education in the sixteenth century was in a state of ferment, as a result of the Humanistic demand for pedagogical reform. Humanism originally grew up outside of the universities, and only later, with difficulty, gained access to their cloisters. Its educational program was based on a core of principles. Firstly, Humanists maintained that education should encourage man in the belief that he can actively form his own nature; secondly, that education should be relevant to man's moral development; thirdly, and related to the two previous points, that man should

seek guidance in the culture of classical antiquity, which, irrespective of its paganism, offered high standards of morality and
intellectual attainment; and fourthly, that each individual should
cultivate a broad spectrum of activities and interests, so as to
become a "universal man."[1]

Huarte's central concern in the *Examen* was with pedagogical
theory and practice, and it is in this context that his treatment of
other issues must ultimately be focused. Via a reconsideration of
basic theoretical principles, he wished to suggest the need to
reform contemporary education. His position with respect to
traditional methods and the challenge of Humanism, however, is
not easy to ascertain. There can be no doubt he was influenced by
the zeal of the Humanists. He shared, to begin with, their desire
for reform. Addressing the King, he writes:

This is what I would have the Academies of your kingdom do: they should
not allow a student to change faculties unless he is good at Latin; and
there should also be examiners to ensure that the student who wishes to
study dialectics, philosophy, medicine, theology, and law has the kind of
wit these disciplines require. If he does not, quite apart from the damage
he will later cause the republic through practicing an art incompetently,
it is a pity to see a man working fruitlessly and racking his brains over
something he finds impossible to master. Because care has not been taken
in this respect in the present day, the Christian religion has been
destroyed by those lacking all aptitude for theology, and public health
undermined by those incapable of practicing medicine. Neither does
jurisprudence enjoy the high standards it should, for the reason that men
do not know which faculty of the soul governs the application and interpretation of the law. (p. 62)

Huarte takes up the same theme in the body of his work: "Imagine somebody entering into our schools in the present day and
carrying out tests of pupils' wits! How many pupils would he have
change disciplines, and how many would he reject completely as
foolish and incapable of learning. And how many would he
reinstate who, though naturally gifted in academic matters, and
in these alone, are forced to pursue humble crafts" (pp. 72–73).
He accepted with the Humanists that a teacher must follow
nature's lead, and cultivate natural aptitudes. Indeed, central to
Huarte's educational program was the belief that the study of the
intellectual powers of each individual was a matter of the utmost

urgency if institutions of education were to function properly and students be efficiently advised and guided.

Huarte also shared the Humanistic conviction regarding man's creative impulse, and was obviously opposed to the traditional emphasis on learning by rote. Indeed, he was even more extreme in this respect than the Humanists, who, because of their concern with correction in the speaking and writing of Latin, often stressed the value of exercising the memory. Huarte felt that the teacher should encourage a questioning, critical attitude in pupils, rather than imitative behavior. It is significant that he also followed the Humanistic emphasis on the importance of having a stimulating environment in which to work, and even advocated that a student should ideally attend a university not in his hometown, in the belief that the family setting is not conducive to academic work (p. 75).

Though stressing the importance of natural ability, Huarte again agreed with the Humanists that the teacher must be of good quality and aware of the enormous responsibility implicit in his role: ". . . all the pupil does, in the way of learning, is to believe everything his master tells him, insofar as he lacks both discretion and mature judgment with which to discern and separate what is false from what is true" (p. 76). Good pupils, of course, are less at the mercy of bad teachers. In addition to having an able teacher, however, the pupil must also cultivate a correct method of studying, to ensure that he does not embark upon new material without a firm basis of necessary knowledge having been acquired (p. 77).

Despite his reforming zeal, it seems that in the long run Huarte moved essentially within the traditional framework of learning. Though he lamented that the gifted often lack the financial means to permit them to dedicate themselves to study, he added significantly that "[s]ince [this] cannot be rectified or avoided, all we can do is to put up with it" (p. 73). He set out to rationalize and perfect formal education as it existed rather than replace it, accepting the traditional view of the aim of education, namely, the producing of experts. The moral, mystical core of Humanism, its vision of the sensitive, all-round man, and its cult of Latin rhetoric, were alien to Huarte. Indeed, to a great extent, his views on education were an outgrowth of his deterministic, materialistic views of man's nature. Hence he was far more extreme than the Humanists in his insistence on the importance of pupil selection. He believed that selection tests are vital prior to the student's commencement of his academic career because without natural ability in a discipline training is of no avail: "I do not deny the power and impact of the good teacher, of skill and application, in cultivating minds, whether these be unsophisticated or able. But what I do maintain is that unless a body has an understanding already pregnant with a firm knowledge of the precepts and rules of that discipline, and of that discipline alone, which he wishes to master, the diligence exhibited by Cicero with his son, and of any other father with his own, will be of no avail" (p. 71). Stated in proverbial terms: ". . . he who goes to Rome a beast, returns a beast: it is of little use to the bumpkin that he go to study at Salamanca . . ." (p. 75). The rules of art and the discipline of education are powerful instruments, but pitted against natural inability they are like giants fighting the gods (p. 79).

Thus, the teacher emerges in Huarte's scheme ultimately with a somewhat diminished role. If a child possesses the right kind of wit, the teacher need only provide the appropriate stimulus, and with the best of his pupils, who enjoy a creative intelligence, this need only be of a superficial kind: "In my view, teachers have no role with respect to their pupils other than that of dictating [basic] doctrine to them; because if these pupils have lively minds, with these alone they will generate incredible concepts . . ." (p. 71). Careful attention must be paid to the age of the pupil, for, over and above a person's unique natural disposition, his wit is conditioned by age (pp. 78, 87). The child is more like an animal than a human being, to the extent that he is ruled by instinct. In adolescence, men slowly begin to perfect their capacity for reason, a capacity which increases throughout their youth. Maturity, however, encompassing as a general rule the period between age thirty and forty, marks the peak of man's development.

Huarte's insistence on natural ability radically contradicts the Humanistic view that the individual, with the teacher's help, can actively perfect himself. Such perfectibility was possible, in Huarte's view, strictly within the circumscribed sphere of a person's nature. It made, of course, little sense to him to reward academic excellence, insofar as he believed that pupils achieve what their innate potentiality allows. This meant that he had in the long run no place for the ideal of the "universal man," which implied the kind of all-round ability he held to be impossible. He confesses as much in the opening lines of his "proemio" to the King:

In order that artificers perform with the skill necessary to the well-being of the republic, it seemed to me, most Catholic Majesty, that there should be passed a law that prevents the carpenter from doing what is properly the laborer's job, and the weaver the architect's, and that prohibits the lawyer from curing the sick and the doctor from practicing law. It should be established that each man should exercise only that art for which he has a natural aptitude, and should leave the rest alone. I have always maintained, on considering how a man's wit is only suited to one discipline, that nobody can practice two arts equally well. Measures should be taken to prevent people making a mistake when choosing their profession. Deputies should be appointed in the republic, individuals of great prudence and knowledge, who could establish what kind of a wit a person has when he is very young, thereby making him study only that discipline for which he is suited, and not leaving it to a matter of choice. Your kingdom would come to possess, merely as the result of matching natural talent with the appropriate discipline, the best artificers in the world and the artifacts of greatest perfection. (pp. 61–62)

The "universal man" corresponded with his "temperate man," of whom he had found only one example in Spain (p. 289). The nearest approximation to the genuine all-rounder was the individual who combined great understanding with some memory and imagination, but even such a person as this was very rare (p. 309). Huarte implies that both types are, in fact, too few in number to undercut his plea for specialization or to be worth taking into consideration in a generalized study of human psychology. In any case they encompass people who tend to be mediocre in their accomplishments (p. 424).

Convinced that each of the sciences requires a man with an appropriate wit, Huarte then proceeded to their categorization in terms of the three faculties of the mind. The memory is best suited to grammar, Latin and other languages, the theory of jurisprudence (i.e., the learning of laws), positivist theology (i.e., the learning of the Scriptures), cosmography (i.e., geography and history), and branches of arithmetic; the understanding to Scholastic theology, the theory of medicine, dialectics, natural philosophy, (i.e., physics, chemistry, biology), moral philosophy, and the practice of jurisprudence; and the imagination to subjects based on harmony and proportion, which include poetry, eloquence, music, preaching, the practice of medicine, mathematics, astrology, kingship, military strategy, painting, tracing, writing, reading, and the inventing of artifacts. Having established this general framework, the author of the *Examen* proceeded to substantiate his system with a detailed discussion.

II *The Categorization of the Sciences*

A. *Language*

With the rediscovery of antiquity, Renaissance scholars once again returned to the debate begun by the Greeks as to whether language is natural or conventional, that is to say, whether there exists an innate, inherent relationship between word and thing, or whether words are imposed according to the arbitrary whim of man. Plato and Aristotle were traditionally associated with these respective viewpoints.[2] Renaissance scholars generally agreed that man had a natural faculty of language, but disagreed as to the status of languages themselves. Some maintained that certain languages were also natural, but the general view was that most, if not all, known languages were conventional.[3] Increasingly, however, scholars began to rebel against the arbitrariness implicit in the conventionalist view, and sought a rational basis in language. This rationalist thesis constituted a more sophisticated version of the naturalist standpoint (which was discredited in its simplistic form).[4] It is usually associated with the Latin grammarian Francisco Sánchez "el Broncense," yet Huarte, whose contribution to linguistic scholarship has unfortunately been disparaged, anticipated Sánchez in this respect.[5]

We have seen that Huarte places languages in the group of subjects relating to the memory:

In the catalogue of the sciences which we said belonged to the memory we included Latin and all the other languages spoken in the world. To this [categorization] no wise man can object, because languages were an invention made by men in order to communicate with each other and explain to each other their concepts, without there being involved any mystery or natural principle. The first inventors merely got together and, according to their own whim, as Aristotle said, established words and gave to each its meaning. From this there resulted so many words and idioms, lacking all rhyme or reason, that without this faculty [i.e., the memory] men would have been unable to understand one another. (pp. 164–65)

He suggests several reasons in support of this Aristotelian, conventionalist view of languages as tied to the memory. Firstly, childhood, when the memory is strong and the understanding weak, is the best age for learning languages. Secondly, a man born deaf is necessarily dumb because he has never heard language and is therefore unable to store it in his memory. And thirdly, the sciences can be taught in any language, authors naturally having recourse to their mother tongue (pp. 165–66). Thus, Huarte concludes, language is something that is *not* connected with reason: "Languages, according to Aristotle, cannot be derived from reason, nor do they consist of discourse or ratiocination . . ." (p. 165).

Later, however, Huarte returns to the subject of language and modifies his views considerably. Drawing the reader's attention to his previously stated claim that languages are the result of pure whim and fancy on the part of those who invented them, Huarte asks why, if this view is correct, do things written in Latin sound better than in any other language. As if not satisfied with his previous defense of the Aristotelian standpoint, he adds yet another reason in its favor, namely, the fact of linguistic diversity. He now, however, contrasts the conventionalist approach with that of Plato, who, as a naturalist, claims that "there are correct names which signify things naturally, and one needs great perception to discover them . . ." (p. 176). This view, Huarte admits, favors the biblical story of the invention of language, and, moreover, provides an answer to his question concerning the excellence of Latin: ". . . the view of Plato is more correct, because, granted that the first inventors created words at will and as they pleased, theirs was a rational whim, which took into account the sound of the word, the nature of the object named, and the grace and elegance of pronunciation . . ." (p. 177). The inventor of Latin, Huarte tells us, had the same curiosity as a certain writer of novels of chivalry, who desperately sought and eventually found a name that expressed the essence of a giant that figured in one of his novels.

Why did Huarte contradict himself in this way? There can be no doubt that the Platonic thesis was and is intuitively attractive. It figures fleetingly in the *Examen* on several occasions: the frenzied man speaks Latin because he, like Adam, looks to the nature of things in his speech (p. 112); language is the mysterious link between the spiritual and corporeal, and accordingly can put the Devil to flight (p. 155); the fact that *letrado* means in Spanish "man of letters" *and* "lawyer" "must be profoundly significant" (p. 208); biblical language is "very mysterious, full of figures of speech and secret ciphers, recondite and not accessible to all" (p. 210); a woman's name, if it is offensively ugly and ill-sounding, may neutralize her physical attractiveness (p. 278); and the term *ingenio* (wit) is aptly named for reasons explained by Plato (p. 426). There is undoubtedly, however, a more important, fundamental reason for Huarte's dissatisfaction with the Aristotelian view. As a scientist, Huarte sought the causes of things, and must have felt ill-at-ease with the notion of language as floating in a conventional, arbitrary limbo, devoid of causes.

B. *Scholastic Theology, Grammar, Rhetoric, and Preaching*

It is Huarte's conventionalist views on language that govern his discussion of Scholastic theology and grammar. He maintains that Scholastic theology is based on the understanding, and that, since this faculty is antagonistic to the memory, "it does not generally happen that an individual is both a great Latinist and a leading Scholastic" (p. 166). Since the great theologians, like Aquinas and Duns Scotus, were concerned with content, not with form, they wrote in a "very dull and ordinary Latin" which naturally scandalizes people who are sensitive to the cadences of Cicero. Huarte illustrates these claims with two stories. The first concerns a theologian who, when requested by his critical pupils to improve his bad Latin, became so inhibited in his thought and experienced such a linguistic crisis that he was finally reduced to speaking in the vernacular (p. 167). The second story relates how Pope Pius IV requested an interview with the most learned man on the Council of Trent, who happened to be a Spaniard, and was somewhat surprised (unlike Huarte) when the Spanish ambassador had to help out his learned compatriot with his own Latin.

By Huarte's time, Humanism was largely exhausted as an intellectual movement, and was tending toward a sterile, prescriptive cultivation of Latin. Not surprisingly, therefore, the author of the *Examen* presented the "grammarians" as strong in the faculty of memory, and committed to a superficial cultivation of eloquence and stylistic excellence in Latin composition. He affirms that rhetorical skill is *not* a sign of intelligence, as ordinary people believe, but that it is in fact wholly antagonistic to the understanding. This explains why Aristotle, Plato, and Hippocrates should have had such barbarous styles and written with such obscurity (p. 180). The true nature of rhetoric is confirmed, Huarte believes, if we consider its role in religion. In the early days of Christianity, the Church's leaders wisely avoided the charms of eloquence, and spoke and preached with simplicity and conviction. Unfortunately, their example has not been followed, and with catastrophic results:

The sterile eloquence and verbosity of German, English, Flemish, French, and other theologians of the North brought about the perdition of their Christian congregations with so much linguistic expertise, so much elaborateness and elegance in preaching, insofar as they [the theologians] lacked understanding to attain the truth. . . . And thus they [those with a strong imagination] worked at interpreting the Divine Scriptures in a way that chimed with their natural inclinations, giving the uneducated to understand that priests can marry, and that there is no need for Lent and fasting, and that it is not right to confess the sins we commit against God. (pp. 199, 201)

If we consider Huarte's views on the above disciplines alongside his views on language(s), it becomes apparent that, like most of his contemporaries, he saw language and thought as largely separate. As R. A. Hall, Jr, writes regarding Renaissance linguistics: "The connection between language and thought . . . was conceived of as being quite loose, and language and thought as being easily separable and distinct."[6] Renaissance scholars believed that, whatever the diversity of languages, thought and creative intellectual activity took place at a pre-verbal level, and its processes were universal and untouched by languages. It is accordingly the understanding which, in the context of Huarte's theoretical framework, has the capacity to "produce within itself and give birth to an offspring, which natural philosophers call an image or concept, which is *verbum mentis*" (p. 427). Naturally, Huarte and his contemporaries had only the most fleeting notion of the subconscious, an essential ingredient of modern linguistic theories which stress man's linguistic creativity. To this extent, their views on language are irredeemably "shallow," within a psychological framework which, in itself, attributed little "depth" to the mind. Hence I feel bound to maintain that recent attempts to present Huarte as a precursor of modern linguistic theories[7] are misleading.

C. *Law, Medicine, and Government*

Huarte's discussion of law, medicine, and the art of government clearly illustrates the difficulty he experienced in adhering to a strict categorization of the sciences on the basis of the three faculties of the mind, a difficulty which was only partially offset by his drawing a basic division between the theoretical and practical branches of disciplines. For example, he insists initially on the *rationality* of the laws by which a society is run, and the need to avoid arbitrariness in their application at all costs. The role of king or emperor is strictly that of the upholder of the law. As Huarte writes:

The law, carefully considered, is nothing more than the rational will of the legislator, through which he [the legislator] explains the manner in which he wishes to be decided the everyday cases which occur in his state, so as to maintain his subjects in peace and teach them how they should live and conduct themselves. I said *rational* will, because it does not suffice for the king and the emperor, who are the efficient cause of the law, to explain their will in any manner they choose, in order that it become law; because if this will is not just and reasonable it cannot be called, nor is it, law, in the same way that we could not consider any creature to be a man that did not possess a rational soul. And thus it is the practice that kings make their laws in consultation with the wise and learned, so that these laws should be correct, fair, and good, and the subjects accept them willingly and feel obliged to respect them and abide by them. (pp. 208–209)

From this, Huarte concludes it is the memory and not the understanding that needs to be operative in judicial matters (pp. 210–11).

However, mature consideration suggested to Huarte that his arguments apply to the theory, rather than to the practice, of law. Experience, he notes, teaches us that the application of laws to complex, concrete situations demands subtle interpretation:

. . . although it is true that the law should be as we have defined it, it rarely happens that things are as straightforward in reality as the understanding pretends. It is not always possible for the law to be just and rational, and provide for all possible contingencies. Nor is it always possible to present it clearly and unambiguously, because, when all is said and done, it was established by human convention, and this convention cannot foresee all that will happen. Experience shows that, once a law has been carefully formulated, it needs, in a short while, to be recast because, when it is made public and put into practice, a thousand drawbacks in it are discovered, none of which were anticipated when it was being drawn up. (pp. 212–213)

Actual application of the law requires a good understanding, particularly when we consider the fundamental instability of man's reason (p. 224). Huarte found the lack of any absolute criterion of judgment, troubling though it was generally to the intellectual, doubly so in matters of human justice.

A similar problem arose regarding medicine. It was clear to Huarte that the medical student should receive a good training in medical techniques, and that such a training would ideally require both understanding and memory. He was equally convinced, however, that a knowledge of man in the abstract by no means sufficed in the task of healing the sick, and that in this context the doctor's most valuable attributes were a good imagination and great practical experience:

Hence it is certain that it is the imagination that acquaints us with particular things, and passes judgment upon them, and not the understanding or exterior senses; from which it follows that the doctor who is well versed in theory, through excelling either in the understanding or in the memory, will necessarily be a poor practitioner, because of the deficiency he must have with respect to the imagination; on the other hand, the man who is to distinguish himself as a practitioner will necessarily be a bad theoretician, because a strong imagination cannot be joined to the understanding or memory. And this is the reason why no man can be truly consummate in medicine or fail to make mistakes in his diagnoses; because in order to practice well he needs to have both a sound knowledge of the basic principles and to have a good imagination with which to put them into practice; and, as I have shown, these two things are incompatible. (p. 233)

Huarte's complete abandonment of his system of categorization occurs with respect to the question of the qualities necessary in a good prince, who, he confesses, does need a perfectly balanced temperament: ". . . in this [temperament] the basic qualities exist in such weight and proportion that heat does not exceed cold, nor humidity dryness. Rather they are found in such balance and conformity as if they were not diametrically opposed or naturally contrasting. We have as a result an instrument so suited to the tasks of the rational soul that man comes to possess a perfect memory for things past, a great imagination to see what lies in the future, and also a sound understanding with which to distinguish, infer, reason, judge, and select" (p. 288). People possessing such a temperament are rare, but are distinguished by certain characteristics by which they may be recognized (p. 289 ff.). Huarte tactfully arranged that these characteristics should be precisely those possessed by the ruling monarch of Spain, Philip II. The extent to which this was a tactical ploy, to gain protection and favor, may be gauged by the fact that, in the posthumous revised edition of his work, he felt free to state categorically, in a manner more consistent with the whole theoretical basis of the *Examen*, that men with a perfect temperamental balance are inclined to mediocrity (p. 424).

D.   *The Art of Military Strategy*

The subject of military strategy provided Huarte with a framework in which he was able to debate certain issues of central importance in Golden Age culture and about which, as one would anticipate, he held incisive and original views. There was, to begin with, the traditional dispute regarding the relative merits of the pen and the sword. Huarte was aware of the widespread tendency to exalt military prowess above all else (pp. 253–54). However, as a man who did not belong to the traditional military aristocracy and whose life was dedicated to the peaceful pursuit of intellectual truth, he himself inevitably viewed military life with somewhat qualified respect. Not without reason does he note that *malicia* (malice) resembles *milicia* (militia), thus associating military expertise with the suspect faculty of the imagination (pp. 254–55, 257). Moreover, he significantly suggests that those people attracted to arms be excluded from universities, which are reserved for those in whom the understanding is dominant (p. 355). He willingly confesses that intellectuals are unsuited to warfare by virtue of their cowardice.

The second important subject that Huarte discussed with reference to military strategy was that of Fortune. He reviews the history of the concept in Stoic philosophy, in which it was embodied in the person of a fickle Goddess, who tended to favor the wicked and persecute the good (pp. 266–67). Though noting the popularity of the concept in folk ideology, Huarte can find no place for it in his own philosophy. Military art is like a game of chess, he explains, in which the whole notion of luck, good or bad, is superfluous (pp. 269–70). The winner is the man who best exploits the tricks that lead to victory, who, in short, applies the best stratagem in a given situation. He will be, furthermore, a man in whom the imagination, as opposed to the understanding, is strong. All one needs to do is to learn the rules of the game and apply them with skill in a given situation. Hence, "we must speak of the victorious captain as being wise and the man that he conquers foolish, not as being fortunate and unfortunate respectively" (p. 270).

The metaphor of chess and value of individual initiative lead Huarte on to the third important subject, namely, that of *hidalguía* (nobility). The fact that the pawn can eventually become a queen suggests to Huarte the value of social mobility and of basing social prestige on proven individual worth (p. 272). Huarte was at pains to insist that ultimately all nobility is a gift of the king, as a reward for personal initiative. Perhaps his own suspect blood encouraged him to see nobility as lying mainly in "the valor of the individual himself," rather than in riches and antiquity of lineage, which in themselves are "of little import" (p. 277).

The negative aspects of Huarte's pedagogical program seem clear enough. To begin with, it is impossible to escape the conclusion that he encouraged many features of traditional education that were detrimental to the development of science. Though he admitted the importance of both theory and practice, so inextricably intertwined in scientific pursuit, he himself certainly esteemed the former, and his categorization of the sciences and his theory of human psychology suggested that an individual must choose positively to follow a particular discipline in the light of his own natural endowment. Huarte was also scornful of manual work, which he does not include at all in his classification, and associates the invention of artifacts with the suspect imagination (p. 164). He had no vision of technological progress, despite his emphasis on progress in the arts and sciences, or indeed any interest in technology itself. In his own discipline of medicine, university lecturers left dissection to assistants plying the humble trade of surgeon, and Huarte did nothing to discourage this system. Finally, he was insensitive to the importance of mathematics.

On the positive side, however, Huarte not only included in his work many pieces of good, practical advice for teacher and student but may be said to have made a major contribution to that eternal question of nature-versus-nurture, as it is nowadays known. Modern scholars have continued to consult the *Examen* in this context and to find it stimulating reading.[8] Moreover, there is in Huarte a serious commitment to intellectual endeavor which it is impossible not to admire. Turning away from the barren literary pretentiousness of the Humanists, he saw education as being concerned with the cultivation of the intellect and man's powers of ratiocination. Finally, his comments regarding certain disciplines show him to possess a penetrating mind, capable of generating fascinating and challenging insights into a wide variety of issues.

CHAPTER 8

Toward a Brave New World

I *Eugenics and Dietetics*

THE final chapter of the *Examen*, which treats a number of topics relating to an area of science now covered by genetics, is possibly the most difficult to evaluate in the whole book, in that it constitutes the most modern and, at the same time, most outmoded section of Huarte's work. This paradox is complicated by the fact that, whereas elsewhere Huarte emerges as a precursor of various modern humanistic ideals, he anticipates in this context some of the aspects of modern applied science whose nightmarish possibilities have haunted the twentieth century, and which are generally associated with the evils of totalitarian society. We need both to understand the above paradox, and to relate the concluding chapter of the *Examen* to Huarte's total vision of the identity of man.

Huarte set out in his discussion of human intelligence with one basic aim: to reform current practice in education and thereby benefit society. Yet confident as he was of the power of education in the formation of individual character, and attentive as he was to the subtleties of pedagogical technique, he looked finally to man's natural attributes as the deciding factor in human behavior. Such a perspective did not lead, in Huarte's case, to a passive acceptance of the rule of nature. The physician believed that scientific understanding was above all a basis for controlling the universe. "Natural" was not synonymous with "God-given." Thus, having established the fundamental importance of man's innate endowment, the author of the *Examen* set out to suggest ways in which we can influence the generation of this endowment so as to produce intelligent children.

The logic of Huarte's views is irrefutable. The intellectual attributes of a child depend, he argued, on the physical makeup of

99

the body. This physical makeup is, in part, hereditary, being conditioned by the seed of both male and female. He concluded that, although it may be impossible to influence radically an individual wit once acquired, it should be possible to control the manner of acquisition in such a way as to produce any desired end:

It is a truly astounding fact that, although Nature is, as we know her to be, prudent, clever, and of great artifice, wisdom, and power, and a man a work over which she took such great pains, for every prudent, wise man she makes, she produces an infinite number devoid of intelligence. Seeking the reason and natural causes to account for this phenomenon, I have myself discovered that parents do not go about the sexual act with the care and attention that Nature requires, nor do they know the procedures they should follow if they are to produce prudent, intelligent children. Because for the same reason as in any region, temperate or intemperate, one man is born intelligent, a hundred thousand could be born, if the same sequence of causes is followed. If this could be achieved by art, we would have performed the greatest possible service for the republic. (p. 310)

There was no doubt in Huarte's mind that failure by intelligent parents to produce intelligent children must be explained in terms of ignorance regarding proper breeding. Overcoming his natural modesty regarding such delicate matters, therefore, he undertook to outline a scheme for sexual orientation. He divides his discussion into four basic sections, which deal with: (1) the temperament necessary in men and women in order to be able to procreate; (2) how to procreate boys as opposed to girls; (3) how to procreate intelligent as opposed to foolish children; (4) postnatal care and the maintenance of intelligence in the newly born.

Huarte begins by assuming a considerable degree of physiological identity between men and women: "To such an extent is this true that if, after having made a perfect man, nature should wish to change him into a woman, she need only place the sexual organs within the body . . ." (p. 315). Striking a misogynist note which will pervade the closing sections of his work, Huarte seems to suggest that women should be considered as basically imperfect versions of men. The delicate balance between the sexes is confirmed by the existence of effeminate, homosexual men ("who generally fall into the basest of sins" [p. 316]) and masculine women. Such facts are confirmed by experience, and experience "admits of no dispute or argument" (p. 316).

Despite his professed desire to remain close to observable fact, Huarte undertook a study of men and women on the basis of the classical theory of the elements, which was to lead him to some bizarre conclusions. He applied his accustomed technique, presenting man as a microcosm, the functioning of whose body is to be explained in terms of the physical laws of the macrocosm. Hence, for example, he concluded that just as the seeds of plants flourish best in moist, cold ground, such as Northern Europe (England, Flanders, and Germany), so human seed flourishes best in a woman who is cold and moist. However, these qualities should not be found in an extreme form: ". . . although it is true that a woman should be cold and moist in order to conceive, she can be so to such an extent that the seed is drowned, just as we see that wheat is ruined by too much rain and prevented from ripening by extreme cold" (p. 317). This leads Huarte on to attempt a classification of women in terms of their reproductive capacities. Three major classes or grades emerge in accordance with certain degrees of cold and humidity, each grade being specified on the basis of intelligence, behavior, voice quality, weight, skin-color, degree of body hair, and degree of physical atractiveness. Hence, the first grade includes women who are sharp of wit, rough in behavior, deep-voiced, light in weight, dark-skinned, hairy, and ugly. Women of the second grade are of average intelligence, normal in behavior, have moderately pitched voices, are of average weight, have fair skin, blond hair, and are very beautiful. Women of the third grade are of low intelligence, well-behaved, have high-pitched voices, are heavily built, very fair-skinned, blond, and beautiful.

Men also admit of three different grades. Those of the first grade, who have good memories, are unassertive, have high-pitched voices, a light build, fair skin, fair hair, and are handsome. Those of the second grade, in whom the understanding is strong, are sympathetic, easy-going, average with respect to voice pitch and weight, of normal skin- and hair-coloring, and reasonably handsome. Those of the third grade, who have a dominant imaginative faculty, are intelligent, proud, deep-voiced, muscular, dark-skinned, hirsute, and ugly.

Having concluded that a couple's ability to procreate children depends upon the proper balance of the elements, Huarte is able to offer positive advice concerning the correct pairing of men and women. For example: "[A woman of the third grade] should marry a man who is hot and dry according to the third degree, because his seed is so seething and effervescent that, for it to stick and take root, it must fall into a very cold, humid spot; this kind of seed resembles watercress insofar as it can only germinate in water" (p. 329).

Having discussed to his satisfaction the question of fertility, Huarte next turned his attention to the problem of how to conceive boys as opposed to girls. This problem arises logically from the attempt to produce the most intelligent children, for Huarte, as we have seen, shared the widespread misogynism of his day:

Parents who wish to be blessed with children who are intelligent and gifted academically should try and have boys, since girls, on account of the cold and humidity of their female constitution, cannot attain great intelligence. We observe merely that they speak with the appearance of ability on trivial, superficial matters, in ordinary (albeit very contrived) language. When confronted by academic work, they can only learn a little Latin, and this because it is a matter of memory. We should not blame them for their gross limitations, but rather the cold and humidity which is an integral part of their female nature, that is, those qualities which, as we have shown, are antagonistic to intelligence and ability. (p. 331)

Differences of sex relate, in Huarte's view, to crucial differences between a man's testicles, the right testicle being hot and dry, and the left, cold and wet. In the early history of mankind, this resulted in women always producing twins, one male and one female, whereby the population was increased with maximum economy. This pristine balance has been lost in the modern world, however, where seven females are now born for every male: "From which we may deduce that either nature is very tired or that there exists some impediment as a result of which she is prevented from functioning as she would wish" (p. 333).

On this basis, Huarte laid down certain instructions which, he confidently predicted, would lead to the production of a male child. These instructions were as follows: parents should eat cold, dry food; digest well; have lots of exercise; not copulate until the seed is mature; copulate just before the woman's period[1]; and ensure that the seed falls on the righthand side of the womb.

The section concerning the producing of intelligent children begins on a negative note, namely, the impossibility of offering a totally adequate and comprehensive scientific description of the processes involved. This hesitancy is somewhat surprising; the author of the *Examen* is not normally given to modesty in his appraisal of the adequacy of rational explanation. However, the loss of confidence is momentary. Huarte immediately argues that, in the absence of scientific guidance, we should not have recourse to astrology. The crucial factor is not the ascendency of planets but the physical forces operative at the moment of conception: ". . . the stars affect the child superficially, imparting heat, cold, humidity, and dryness, but providing no substance on which these qualities might rest throughout his life, as do the four elements, fire, earth, air, and water . . ." (p. 343). That is to say, the most important thing in the generation of children is to ensure that the correct elements are present, ". . . because these [elements] will always maintain the same balance of weight and quantity in the composite nature of any 'mixed' thing, independent of the movement of the skies" (p. 344). The elements enter into play via the seed and menstrual blood, which they constitute and which are the basic components of generation. The elements depend in turn, of course, on the food we eat. Hence it follows that, if parents are to procreate intelligent children, they must eat certain kinds of food. Those that are cold and dry (e.g., bread) favor the understanding; those that are wet (e.g., trout), the memory; and those that are hot (e.g., vinegar), the imagination.

It is worthwhile to note that, whatever the general trend of his theory of genetic engineering and its relationship to unsavory modern theories, Huarte himself saw major obstacles to the generation of a race of supermen. Wise men, he argued, are not often blessed with intelligent sons, and for reasons that are easy to explain: ". . . the rational faculty is antagonistic to the choleric, concupiscent faculty, in such a way that if a man is wise he cannot also be brave, of great physical strength, a hearty eater, and sexually very potent; because the natural dispositions which are necessary if the rational soul is to function properly are the direct opposite of those required by the choleric, concupiscent faculty" (p. 353). In such cases the woman's seed is dominant.

The chapter concludes with a section on postnatal care— various pieces of advice to parents, such as the need to wash the newly born in warm, salty water, and to find a wet-nurse whose elemental makeup is suitable.

II *A Scientific Mythology*

It is apparent that Huarte's remarks on human breeding and his advocating of what we would now call genetic engineering were no mere adjunct to his work, constituting an unfortunate incrustation on an otherwise impeccably tasteful philosophy. They are rather eloquent of the pervasive deterministic bias of his whole work. He was no flincher, and once caught up in the logic of an argument, he pursued it to its conclusion with a persistence, vigor, and single-mindedness it is impossible not to admire, but which is sometimes a little unnerving. Having established to his satisfaction the existence of certain categories of intelligence, and scientifically explained the reason for their existence, it seemed to Huarte a natural conclusion to his theories to suggest ways in which man's active involvement in their production might be attained. Here, as elsewhere, his ideas, once translated into the language of twentieth-century science, reveal a startling modernity and richness of insight.[2]

Yet we need to tread with care here. There is a gap that is more than merely verbal between Huarte's knowledge and the science of the modern world. The very fact that genetics was an unknown science to the Renaissance points to the necessary poverty of Huarte's intellectual equipment in this direction, a poverty so basic and all-encompassing that the whole intellectual edifice he constructed in this area has a somewhat oblique relationship to reality. The fact is he just did not have the conceptual apparatus adequate for the task before him. He himself, of course, was blissfully unaware of this deficiency. The human body was for him an essentially non-mysterious entity. He saw it as just a part of the natural universe and subject to the same physical laws. The physical sciences provided both the concepts and techniques for investigation, and to extend them to the study of the human body seemed both natural and straightforward.

It would perhaps have been better for Huarte's reputation if he had never written the final chapter of his work. Much of it is not only completely misguided but now appears frankly silly. Consider, for example, his view that, because the female seed can sometimes dominate the male, women can become pregnant with the seed of animals after being sexually assaulted by them ("a fact which many authentic stories affirm" [p. 358]) and yet produce perfectly normal offspring. It is tempting, in view of such passages, to bypass the final chapter of the *Examen*, so much of which has an air of unreality. This procedure would be incorrect, however. Firstly, it represents the logical culmination of Huarte's ideas, and can be said to anticipate, quite brilliantly in certain respects, modern ideas on genetic engineering. Secondly, when the historian of science comes to consider what is wrong-headed in the *Examen,* it should be clear that it is not his task to sift the intellectual tradition for currently acceptable views which bear upon the concerns of modern scholarship. We may learn as much from the errors of the past as from its successes. Finally, to limit one's attention to the modern aspects of Huarte's work and to ignore its more benighted ideas is to present a distorted image of the physician's total intellectual vision. It may bolster the scientists' pride to see the history of science as a gradual rise to the present summit of excellence, but this does not do justice to the facts. The full picture provides a salutary reminder that science has frequently regressed or gone up blind alleys.[3]

In final analysis, the last chapter of the *Examen* represents a classic case of the presentation of a brilliant thesis at a time when science itself was not sufficiently advanced to be able to test and articulate it. Huarte's assumption that exploration and explanation of the microcosm must proceed along the same lines as that of the macrocosm was in principle sound enough, but he was naturally unaware of just how shaky were the foundations of the physics, chemistry, and physiology of his day. Moreover, he proceeded to apply these sciences to the problems of genetics and sexual reproduction with a naïveté that is frequently disarming. His inability to recognize the limitations of his knowledge led him into a fantasy-land of his own making, thereby demonstrating quite clearly that science has its own mythology, and that it is often no more grounded in fact than are the mythologies of religion and literature.

CHAPTER 9

The Influence of the Examen

I Spain

A. Scientific and Technical Literature

IT is impossible in the present study, for reasons of space, to deal with all the numerous writers who, in the period immediately following the publication of the *Examen*, registered the impact of the ideas of Juan Huarte. References to him are often fleeting, some scholars being confessedly interested only in certain aspects of his work. This applies to authors of books on the subject of nobility, such as Benito Guardiola[1] and Bernabé Moreno de Vargas,[2] who seem to have found Huarte's discussion of *hidalguía* extremely informative. Similarly, students of medicine often defined their own standpoints in the light of theories outlined in the *Examen*. Andrés Velázquez, for example, found his principal modern source of information in Huarte. He notes, to take but one instance, that Huarte supported the view that children learn easily because of their humid temperament: ". . . Huarte declared this to be so, with great skill and erudition, as he does in everything with which he deals."[3] However, he is disturbed by the freedom with which Huarte criticizes the ancients, particularly Galen; and believes he was wrong over specific issues, such as the cause of laughter, and the ability of the uneducated to utter spontaneously words of wisdom.[4]

It seems true to say that, despite frequent references to the *Examen*, those who criticized or supported Huarte's theories lacked his breadth of vision and failed to encompass the grand design of his achievement. The possible single exception to this trend was Diego Alvarez, whose work appears to have contained an analysis of Huarte's total philosophy but which has unfortunately been lost.[5] Though Huarte had himself been one of the early campaigners for rational procedure, ironically his influence declined as the seventeenth century drew to a close and the Enlightenment began. Scholars became too fired by the achievements of contemporary science and too concerned with the future to take the *Examen* seriously, aspects of which were certainly by this time coming to seem very antiquated. Feijóo found it virtually impossible to acquire a copy of the work.[6] References to Huarte in this period are few, although some continued to be favorable. His ability to speak to a different age is confirmed by Ignacio Rodríguez, who was particularly fascinated by Huarte's doctrine of creativity. Significantly, however, he applies it in a context that would have seemed strange to the physician, namely, to technological progress: "It is evident that nobody served as a teacher for those people who discovered gunpowder and invented artillery, printing, clocks, and other infinite secrets of the arts. . . ."[7] Moreover, possibly under the influence of Romanticism, Rodríguez associates creativity much more firmly than did Huarte with the faculty of the imagination, and, in explicit opposition to the doctrine of the *Examen*, claims that the inventive spirit of man knows no national boundary, and can be found in what are believed to be backward nations.[8]

B. *Literary Theory and Criticism*

Huarte's attitude to imaginative literature is somewhat ambivalent. On the one hand, he speaks disparagingly of those men whose imaginative faculty is so strong that they "lose themselves in novels of chivalry, in Orlando, Boscán, in Diana de Montemayor and similar things . . ." (p. 170); and he claims, in view of the mutual antagonism between poetry and the understanding, that "a man who is sane and in his right mind cannot be a poet . . ." (p. 169). On the other hand, however, he firmly associates poetry with the third of man's wits, the creative wit, which he presents as the source of the poet's elevated words and maxims (p. 433). Where he disagreed with Plato was in the attribution of a divine origin to such creativity. Much more to Huarte's liking was Aristotle's explanation of poetic invention in terms of temperamental imbalance of a physical nature.

Despite its inconsistencies and contradictions, the *Examen* seems to have been read enthusiastically by contemporary literary writers and critics. Its influence exercised itself in three main ways: firstly, in the explication of the Platonic divine afflatus by

reference to purely physiological factors; secondly, in the associa-
tion of the poetic faculty with the imagination; and thirdly, in the
rise of *conceptismo*.

It is perhaps not surprising to find Spain's leading theorist of
literature, Alonso López Pinciano, taking up Huarte's attempt to
provide a scientific, rational explanation of literary creativity.
Pinciano was a medical doctor by profession, in which capacity
he would certainly have been familiar with the *Examen*. He
followed Huarte's example in maintaining that all human activity, including creative writing, can be explained by reference to
the natural sciences, and he developed his own theoretical concepts in terms of a strictly deterministic, empirical view of the
human mind.[9]

Pinciano was not the only literary critic in Spain to find inspiration in the *Examen*. Huarte's ideas were also taken up by the
Sevillian school of poetry of the late sixteenth century, whose
most distinguished representative was perhaps Luis Carvallo.
Carvallo cites Huarte by name on several occasions, and it is clear
that many of his ideas and even much of his phraseology derive
from the latter's work. He stresses that poetry is not born of "art"
but of "natural inclination"; that each wit is suited to only one
science; that poetic creativity should be explained in strictly
somatic terms; and that poetry is born of the imagination.[10]
Unlike Huarte, however, Carvallo is passionately persuaded of
the value of imaginative literature, and is, therefore, more in-
convenienced than the author of the *Examen* by the supposed antagonism between the imagination and the understanding. Not
surprisingly, he attempts to carve out a role for the understanding
in literary activity, even to the point where he values the poet for
the great insights he achieves on a purely intellectual level.[11]

The possible influence of Huarte on Baltasar Gracián was suggested by A. F. G. Bell,[12] and considered in some detail by C. M.
Hutchings.[13] Though he fails to mention Huarte explicitly, common sense suggests that Gracián would certainly have familiar-
ized himself with the physician's work while undertaking his own
study of man's creative wit, and, indeed, there are obvious
similarities between the two writers. Like Huarte, Gracián insists
upon the importance of natural ability, as opposed to training,
and concedes that a man's nature changes during the course of his
life, as the balance of his humors shifts. Though the sharing of
such traditional, commonplace views is not in itself sufficient
proof of direct contact, its significance is enhanced when we con-

sider that Gracián follows Huarte's false derivation of "ingenio"
from "ingenerare," and adopts almost word for word Huarte's
definition of the arts and sciences.[14]

Such similarities, however, must not blind us to the real differences between the two writers. Although both saw the mind as
a generator of concepts, it seems that concepts meant different
things to them. Huarte saw the concept as a mental counterpart
of the entities of the external world (p. 427), whereas for Gracián
it was "an act of the understanding, which expresses the correspondence that exists between objects."[15] Gracián's "concept,"
therefore, has more in common with Huarte's "analogy" ("com-
paración"). And it is here, perhaps, that we must seek the most
fruitful area of comparison, irrespective of the extent of any
direct contact such as that indicated above.

Initially, it must be confessed, the similarities seem to be of a
limited kind. Whereas Gracián associated the discovery of cor-
respondences with the understanding, Huarte's analogy derived
from the imagination, "because it is a figure, and suggests a good
correspondence and similarity" (p. 194). Nevertheless, Gracián's
"understanding" is not that of discursive reasoning, and, we are
reminded, Huarte and his disciples were somewhat confused
about the respective roles of the imagination and understanding.
What *is* apparent is that both literary writer and scientist saw the
universe as a metaphorical poem, made up of conceits, which,
they believed, must be deciphered and understood, if man is to
understand fully the nature of God's creation. Indeed, the comparison between Huarte and Gracián illustrates that there is
much in common between the literary metaphor and the scientific analogy, in that, at their best, both embody a particular "insight" and "vision." It also reminds us that, whatever the nature
of their relationship in the present age, science and imaginative
literature have enjoyed in the past a rich symbiotic relationship,
and that the disjunction between both that occurred in Inquisitorial Spain was not as complete as might at first seem to
have been the case. However, this is to anticipate the discussion
contained in the following section.

C. *Imaginative Literature*

It would seem possible to relate the *Examen* to imaginative
literature in three basic ways. Firstly, on a relatively trivial level,
Huarte undoubtedly helped provide the conceptual framework

and technical terminology for psychological discussion by intelligent laymen and a background of specialist information familiar to writers. Secondly, he may have been one of the sources of some of the themes and dominant preoccupations of literary works. And, finally, it would seem potentially fruitful to compare the general philosophical position expounded in the *Examen* with those implicit and explicit in imaginative literature. Rather than attempt a general study of the relationship between the *Examen* and Golden Age literature, which would be a rather impractical undertaking in the present context, I have chosen to illustrate my discussion by reference to Miguel de Cervantes, a writer with whom Huarte has often been associated.

The very prologue to *Don Quijote* contains words and phrases reminiscent of the *Examen*. For example, Cervantes describes his book as an "offspring of his understanding," which has been "engendered" by his "wit"[16] (cf. Huarte's "to give birth to an offspring [of the understanding]" [p. 427]). The book recounts the story of a man "full of thoughts numerous and never before imagined"[17] (cf. Huarte's "things so delicate, so true and prodigious, that they have never previously been seen, heard, or written down" [p. 433]). In fact, Cervantes worked entirely in terms of the medical doctrine—physiological and psychological—that was the basis of Huarte's work. Don Quixote's madness, for example, is a classic case study in the Huartean mold, insofar as the knight suffers from a "dried brain." The parallels are so strong at times that some scholars have argued not merely for a community of scholarship but for the direct influence of the *Examen* on Cervantes. Rafael Salillas maintains that the very term "ingenioso" in the title of Cervantes' most famous work derives directly from Huarte.[18] This subject, however, well illustrates the problem in dealing with cases of supposed influence involving the *Examen*. Huarte's work is so permeated by traditional material that unless a writer shows the impact of terms and ideas largely original to the *Examen* it seems dangerous to postulate freely direct contact. In point of fact, Huarte uses the term "ingenioso" relatively infrequently (in comparison to "ingenio") (e.g., pp. 202, 268, 343, 365) and invariably in a somewhat loose, nontechnical manner. Salillas seems to be on firmer ground when he argues the influence of Huarte on *Galatea* regarding the question of "differences of wit."[19]

The above mention of insanity is a reminder, on turning to consider the thematic resemblances between Huarte and Cervantes, that this was a subject of abiding fascination to both writers. Huarte's own attitude to mental imbalance is profoundly ambiguous. He believed that all men are "distempered," but that, precisely because of this infirmity and the fact that they may be foolish in certain respects, they can achieve excellence in one particular field. The first case study he considers is that of Democritus, a man whose understanding had undergone hypertrophy. Democritus' comments were so strange, notes Huarte, that all the inhabitants of his native city considered him to be mad. Hippocrates, however, on being called to attend the supposedly sick man, offered a different diagnosis: ". . . he found that he [Democritus] was the wisest man in the whole world. And thus he said that the madmen and unbalanced people were those who had brought him, since they had formed such an opinion of so prudent a man" (pp. 434–35). Other, modern case studies are cited: the humble rustic who, because of a rise in body temperature, became eloquent (p. 107); the frenetic man who, through a similar excess of heat, and hence of imagination, began to recite verse (pp. 107–108); and the frenetic woman who told people of their virtues and vices and predicted their fortunes with such accuracy that all were scared of her, "fearing the truths that she told" (p. 109). Perhaps the most significant patient, however, is the page-boy:

[He] was considered when sane to be a boy of low intelligence; but on falling ill he uttered so many witticisms, gave such apt replies to the questions people put to him, and described so many ploys he used for governing the kingdom of which he imagined himself to be the lord that, in their amazement, people came from far and wide to see and hear him, and the real lord himself never left his bedside, constantly beseeching God that he not be cured. The reason for this became apparent later. Because once the page had recovered from his illness, the doctor who had been attending him went to take his leave of the lord, hoping to receive some reward or words of praise; but the lord spoke as follows: "I swear by Almighty God, Doctor, that nothing has ever disturbed me more than seeing this page cured; because it was not right to exchange such sparkling insanity for a wit so dull as the one which this boy is blessed with in health. It seems to me that you have turned him from a sane, quick-witted man into a fool, which is the greatest misfortune that can happen to anybody." The poor doctor, on seeing just how unwelcome was his cure, went to say goodbye to the page, who, as their conversation was drawing to a close, remarked: "Doctor, I am truly most grateful for the service you have done me in having restored my sanity, but I swear upon my soul that I am, in a manner of speaking, saddened by being cured, because when I was mad I had the most lofty thoughts and imagined myself to be so great a lord that there was not a king in the land who did not acknowledge me as his liege. And what did it matter if it was a joke and a lie, for it gave the same satisfaction as if it were true. How much worse off am I now, on finding that I am truly a poor page, and that tomorrow I must begin to serve somebody who, when I was ill, I would not have employed as my lackey!" (pp. 108–109)

Such case studies, it will quickly be appreciated, are very relevant to Cervantes' work. Tomás, the eponymous protagonist of the *Licenciado Vidriera*, is possessed by the strange obsession that he is made of glass, and fears the proximity of other men. In spite of, or because of, his delusion, however, Tomás is in other respects a man of wisdom, and people come from far and wide to put questions to him. Similarly, Don Quixote suffers from hypertrophy of a faculty to psychotic proportions, but in his case it is his imagination that is impaired. The illness has left his understanding unaffected, if not enhanced in its capacities, and regarding subjects other than chivalry he shows sound judgment.

For some critics, the resemblance between the treatment of the subject of madness in the *Examen* and that in *Don Quijote*, the *Licenciado Vidriera*, and other works by Cervantes, is sufficient for us to claim a case of direct influence. We must not forget, however, that this theme was generally attractive to Renaissance writers, not to mention its popularity in folklore. Outside of Spain, one thinks of Erasmus (*In Praise of Folly*), and within Spain, for example, Lope de Vega (*La adversa fortuna de Don Bernardo Cabrera*). Doubtless there are many reasons for the theme's popularity. Firstly, it may have been part of a reaction against the peaceful world of the pastoral.[20] Secondly, the madman-protagonist would have been a useful defense against possible Inquisitorial persecution. Thirdly, in an age when thoughtful men were beginning to reconsider their own society more critically, the madman was probably seen as embodying the objective viewpoint of the supreme foreigner or outsider. Fourthly, *converso* writers would find it easy to identify with such a protagonist, on account of their own experience of spiritual solitude. Finally, one seems to sense in such writers as Cervantes and Huarte the conviction that into the cracked mind of the schizophrenic a light may fall that gives rise to insights denied to the sane.

The subject of madness is not the only thematic material that Huarte and Cervantes have in common. For example, Huarte's attack upon the novels of chivalry is reflected in *Don Quijote*, not to mention his discussion of such subjects as the pen-versus-sword, social mobility, honor, and the use of the vernacular as a medium for elevated discourse.[21] One is bound to insist, however, that their common concerns in no way constitute proof of *direct* contact between the two writers, insofar as these concerns are of a highly popular, traditional kind, and can be found in numerous Golden Age works. As with the question of terminology, one looks in vain for some idiosyncratic trait of Huarte that also appears in Cervantes.

Such critical caution does not preclude the possibility of a general comparison. Indeed, it could be argued that scholars have been so concerned with the question of the direct influence of Huarte on Cervantes that they seem to have ignored what is perhaps a potentially more suggestive approach to the two writers, namely, a study of the extent to which they share a common intellectual outlook. In fact, Cervantes explored lines of inquiry in a manner strikingly similar to Huarte. His interest in the subject of insanity, for example, was part of a wider concern with that of reality and illusion. Unlike Huarte, he was not a philosopher or scientist, concerned to establish valid, rational criteria of verification, but he did dramatize in a powerful manner the problem of perspectivism which threatened to paralyze Huarte's whole scientific enterprise.[22] He also agreed with Huarte's solution to the skeptical dilemma based on strict adherence to rationalism, which involved a rejection of explanation by recourse to miracles; and shared the view that each individual has a nature that he is destined to fulfill.[23]

It serves little purpose in this context to think in terms of Cervantes' passive borrowing from the *Examen*. The author of *Don Quijote* actively exploited the material with a depth and penetration all his own. Indeed, the very force of his originality led Américo Castro to conclude that Cervantes' vision of biological and moral determinism was not matched by any contemporary scientist.[24] A detailed study of the *Examen* reveals, however, that

Huarte at least is able to stand alongside Cervantes. It might even be claimed that, in the last resort, his basic stance is the more impressive insofar as the very nature of his discipline forced him more out into the open, unprotected by the mythology of literature. He stood alone, for all to see, with the tiger's tail grasped firmly in his hand. What is certainly undeniable is that both writers share a common philosophy of life, exhibiting that strange combined allegiance to the Church and to a rationalism which relegated religion to a status outside their consciences. Together they constitute a constant challenge to those who assume unflinching, unquestioning orthodoxy on the part of Golden Age writers, and a reminder that two of Spain's finest Renaissance minds were driven by the logic of their views toward a determinism that contrasted starkly with repeated assertions of man's free will.

II   *Italy*

A program for educational reform was central to Humanism, and Italy, the cradle of this movement, was bound to receive the *Examen* with some interest, as an impressive, if controversial, contribution to pedagogical literature. It was translated twice into Italian, by Camillo Camilli in 1582 and by Salustio Gratii in 1604. One scholar who benefited thereby was the Jesuit Antonio Possevino, who, though he refers to the Baeza edition of 1575, intimates that he himself used an Italian translation. Possevino (1534–1611) was one of the most representative figures of the Counter-Reformation, and looked kindly on Spain as the leader of this movement. He realized, however, that Huarte was no shining example of Spanish orthodoxy, and, though he shared the physician's view that man is largely governed by a basically unalterable wit, which educationalists should establish and take into account in the individual's education, he was obviously troubled by the deterministic implications of the *Examen*. Possevino was concerned above all to acknowledge man's ultimate liberty, as exemplified by those great historical figures who had overcome gross natural defects by exercising their willpower. In such a way did Demosthenes overcome his stammer. Possevino explicitly rejects Huarte's view that the formation of man's nature is a mechanical process, and considers the attempt to direct it biologically along certain paths not only a sign of madness but of godlessness. He also objects strongly to Huarte's view, which he correctly identifies as deriving from Galen, that the operation of the temperament is decisive in human behavior. In short, he concedes only inclination, not necessity.[25]

It was doubtless Possevino's strong religious beliefs that also led him to favor the "naturalist" view of language, in opposition to Huarte, whom he interprets as supporting unambiguously the "conventionalist" standpoint. Possevino was also opposed to the Spaniard's view that those learned in Latin are not suited to the theoretical sciences, and he points to the great linguistic skill required in complex argumentation.[26]

The contrast between the two scholars indicates the unfortunate repercussions of the religious schism that divided Europe. There is in the Italian writer a palpable loss of confidence. He was troubled above all by Huarte's willingness to follow reason through to its logical conclusions, excluding all appeal to the divine. He insists at all times that man's wisdom lies in not wishing to know too much. The alternative leads to atheism and to doctrines of the mortality of the soul.

The Italian scholar Antonio Zara, Bishop of Pedena (1574–1621), despite his criticism of Huarte's insistence on the organic nature of the intellect and its relationship to the soul, seems heavily indebted to the Spaniard as regards his views on human psychology. He agrees with the emphasis in the *Examen* on the importance of man's natural ability, and adopts Huarte's categorization of the sciences according to the three faculties. He insists that men are of equal endowment intellectually, and that it is in the brain, ultimately in badly formed sense impressions, that inequalities have their origin.[27]

Alessandro Tassoni travelled to Spain in 1600 as secretary to Cardinal Ascanio Colonna, a visit which seems to have largely aroused in him an intense distaste for that country. His *Pensieri diversi*, which first appeared in 1612, have been explored as regards their relationship with Montaigne's *Essays* and Cervantes' work, but not as regards the *Examen*.[28] This is unfortunate since, not only do Huarte and Tassoni discuss many themes in common and share in some respects a similar general outlook, but Tassoni does refer to the physician's work, whereas he makes no explicit reference to either Montaigne or Cervantes.

Tassoni objected to the opposition that Huarte established between the imagination and the intellect, on which the categorization of the sciences in the *Examen* was based. He argued that, since the intellect speculates only with images derived from the imagination (which in turn derives them from the senses), these two faculties must function together to a considerable extent.[29]

For all his disagreement with Huarte, however, Tassoni seems, unlike Possevino and Zara, to have had much in common with Huarte in his freedom of inquiry and general curiosity about the world. His work lacks the unity of the *Examen*, being, as its title suggests, rather a collection of views on disparate subjects, but they are characterized by an independence of judgment similar to that apparent in the *Examen*. Like Huarte, Tassoni respects Aristotle, but refuses to follow the philosopher blindly and uncritically. It seems significant that Tassoni should stress in a manner very similar to Huarte the fertility and creativity of man's wit and also embrace a similar vision of the gradual progress and perfection of the sciences.[30]

Another Italian who drew extensively on the *Examen* was Juan Imperial (1640). He notes that Huarte followed the Galenic theory concerning the influence of the temperament on the soul and intellect.[31] Like Zara, Imperial is opposed to Huarte's belief in the organicity of the soul, and lends his own support to Aristotle's view that the intellect lacks any physical organ. Throughout his work, however, he does draw extensively on Huarte, although his debt is generally not acknowledged.

III   *France*

The *Examen* was first translated into French in 1580 by Gabriel Chappuys. Chappuys, based in Lyon, was a professional translator of Spanish, Italian, and Latin works. His translation of Huarte's work was done quickly and carelessly, but he was an enthusiastic presenter of the text, and obviously believed the *Examen* would be useful to the Republic.[32]

One scholar who may have benefitted immediately from Chappuy's work was Montaigne, who was in Lyon in 1581, when Chappuy's translation was hot off the press.[33] Montaigne was not unconnected with the Spanish world—he knew a little Catalan—and certainly he may have read the *Examen* in some form. There is little evidence, however, to suggest that Huarte's work exerted any major influence on the French writer. Montaigne had been writing his *Essays* since 1571, publishing the first two books in 1580, although these were subsequently revised. That there are strong parallels between the two men is impossible to deny—for example, they were both skeptical and rationalist in outlook, and stressed the close interdependence between body and soul—but such similarities can be easily explained by their common allegiance to the same sixteenth-century group of natural philosophers. Furthermore, there are notable contrasts in the nature and tone of their works. In particular, Montaigne was fascinated as much by himself as by abstract man, who, for all Huarte's personal anecdotes, was always the decisive object of the Spaniard's own study. Both were from different social backgrounds, in the sense that Montaigne was an aristocrat, a product of private tuition, whereas Huarte was a member of an aspiring lesser aristocracy, and a product of public education. Such differences are clearly discernible in what they wrote.

Nevertheless, the fact remains that Huarte first figures in French literature alongside Bodin and Montaigne, in the work of Guillaume Bouchet, whose *Serées* first appeared in 1584. The aspects of Huarte's work that most interested Bouchet were those on eugenics, fits, and the opposition between the memory and the understanding. Like many other scholars, he seems to have read Huarte with enthusiasm, but without grasping the essence of the *Examen*, namely, the matching of the sciences with different aptitudes.[34]

Pierre Charron, in his *Sagesse* (1601), drew more extensively on the *Examen*. Indeed, his use of the work was a decisive factor in its history in France. Charron never cites Huarte, just as he cites none of the other moderns upon whom he drew, but his debt to the Spaniard is manifest. Though more concerned than Huarte with the moral dimension of human behavior, as opposed to pedagogical theory, Charron shared Huarte's aim of achieving a total view of man. Much of what he had to say on temperament, the classification of sciences, practical eugenics, the organicity of the understanding, and even miracles, is derived from the *Examen*. It is probably true to say that the five editions and twenty reprints that Chappuy's translation underwent in the twenty years after the appearance of *Sagesse* was to a great extent attributable to the reception Charron gave to Huarte's work.

In the first few decades of the seventeenth century Huarte's name appeared in numerous French works, to the extent that the *Examen* achieved something of the status of a classic. However, approaches to the work tended to be selective, emphasizing its scientific rather than practical, pedagogical application. This situation was rectified by Dr. Jourdain Guibelet's *Examen de l'Examen*, which appeared in 1631. Guibelet certainly cannot be accused of lack of comprehensiveness in his treatment of Huarte. Indeed, his is the most massive contribution to Huartean scholarship prior to the modern period. Guibelet gives grudging praise to Huarte in the opening pages of the work, before he sets about the task of demolishing the *Examen's* major theses. The French scholar skillfully plays upon all the weaknesses of Huarte's arguments. He aptly remarks, for example, concerning the Spaniard's view of the soul as both immortal *and* subject in its operations to matter: "It is for the Reader to judge whether these propositions are compatible."[35] Guibelet believes, moreover, that Huarte has underrated the importance of application and diligence in education, and that a child should not be prevented from pursuing a particular discipline for which, it is claimed, he is not *naturally* suited.[36] Also criticized is Huarte's rigid and inflexible categorization of the sciences with respect to the faculties of the mind. These faculties, Guibelet maintains, are not mutually antagonistic and the sciences not incompatible. Interrelationships are intimate and complex.[37] Huarte's contradictory views on the nature of language are also rigorously exposed, and Guibelet's own general criticism of the many versions and manifestations in scholarship of Platonic, naturalist views is in itself not without merit.[38]

Guibelet's criticism was frequently valid, but it was also negative, ill-tempered, and, most important of all, had little effect. In 1634, Vion Dalibray's *Supplement*, that is, a translation of the additions to the *Examen* of 1594, appeared. At the same time Huarte was taken up by the Cartesians. Jean Silhon, Pierre Chanet, and Marin Mersenne, friends and correspondents of Descartes, all knew the *Examen*, both directly and via Charron.[39] We cannot be certain whether Descartes himself was familiar with the work. He read very little, though he confesses to having "seen" Gómez Pereira's *Antoniana Margarita*.[40] For the same reasons as Huarte, he looked to nature itself rather than to books. Nevertheless, if he did not read the *Examen*, he certainly did read Charron's *Sagesse*, and hence was familiar with Huarte's ideas. He would have been most impressed by Huarte's treatment of the unreliability of the senses, his distrust of authority, and his praise of man's creativity. Descartes reiterates Huarte's view that "the assent of many voices is not valid proof for truths which are rather difficult to discover, because they are much more likely to be found by one single man than by a whole people."[41] He may also have taken from Huarte the view that medicine is of crucial importance in human behavior: "The Mind depends so much on the temperament and on the disposition of the organs of the body, that if it is possible to find some means of rendering men as a whole wiser and more dexterous than they have been hitherto, I believe it must be sought in medicine."[42] There are other similarities: both accept the existence of three faculties of the soul; that individual differences are accounted for by the temperament, which is affected among other things by the climate; and that the individual should specialize in a given science. It would in fact be true to say that Cartesianism shared the deterministic bias of Huarte's philosophy, claiming that living organisms, just like dead matter, are governed by the laws of physics. Certainly, it tried to carve out a realm for freedom within the spirit, but the whole drift of its basic theory was toward materialism.[43]

There were, however, radical differences between Huarte and Descartes. The Spanish scholar abandoned the problem of the unreliability of the senses with only a patched-up defense against skepticism, being more interested in science itself than in its philosophical basis. Descartes found much of his certainty in mathematics, and stresses the mathematism of nature, which was a closed world to Huarte. Furthermore, if Huarte felt ill at ease in the realm of the senses, he felt even more so in that of the spirit. Descartes, on the other hand, contrasts the reliability of his intuition, the pure light of the mind, with the uncertainty of the senses. He knows only that he is a thinking being. Unlike Huarte, he begins with the spirit, maintaining that the nature of the mind is easier to know than that of the body.

At the end of this period, the *Examen* was given a fresh face in the translation of Charles Vion Dalibray (1645). Dalibray translated numerous works from Italian and four from Castilian. He had more favorable conditions for translating the *Examen* than did Chappuys, having available among other things Chappuys's own translation. He also took longer than Chappuys, and worked with greater care, though his own version is not without errors. Moreover, he was himself a man of ideas and obviously

much interested in the *Examen*. His translation is preceded by a
spirited defense of Huarte, who, he claims, was not a materialist
and non-Christian, but a scientist, dealing with secondary causes.
Dalibray also includes a personal, and apparently genuine, profession of his own faith. His translation was esteemed in his own
and the following century, and ensured a wide diffusion for the
Examen in the Classical Age.[44]

Circumstantial details would seem to suggest that Pascal knew
the *Examen*. He certainly knew Le Pailleur, who was a close
friend of Dalibray, and Dalibray himself, at the time the translation was being prepared, and Pascal was, of course, an avid
reader.[45] However, despite certain superficial similarities, it is
difficult to imagine two men more opposed in basic outlook and
temperament. Most notably, Pascal's deep religiosity and
mystical sentiments are entirely absent from Huarte, whose commitment to rationalism remained constant.

Although French scholars continued to refer extensively to
Huarte's work throughout the seventeenth century, the
Enlightenment saw a decline in his influence. The spirit of this
age was doubtless not conducive to a sympathetic reading of the
Examen, which must have seemed increasingly repressive and
conservative in outlook. References to Huarte are fewer, and
cases of his influence more quesionable. Pierre Bayle certainly
found a place for him in the *Dictionnaire Historique et Critique*
(1720), but it is doubtful whether Montesquieu drew upon his
theory of climatic determinism, as has sometimes been claimed.[46]

IV *England*

The British Museum has a work entitled *A Triall of Wits*, by
John Wolf, published in London in 1590, which is a fragment of
four leaves and is part of a translation of the *Examen*. The full
English translation by Richard Carew, from the Italian translation by Camillo Camilli, appeared in 1594. A direct translation
from the Spanish was made by Edward Bellay in 1698, extracts of
which were reproduced in *A Treatise of the Education and
Learning Proper for the Different Capacities of Youth* (1734).

The rather indirect passage of the *Examen* into England is indicative of its more restricted impact in this country in comparison to other European countries, although it must be
remembered that a full-scale study has yet to be made. It is tradi-

tionally claimed that Francis Bacon drew his scheme for the categorization of the sciences from Huarte.[47] Several editions of Huarte's work and the English translation had appeared before Bacon's *The Advancement of Learning* (1605), so there is no problem chronologically. Nevertheless, it should be borne in mind that Luis Vives, to name but one scholar, had also suggested the importance of matching individual skills to particular disciplines. It seems that more detailed research is required before any certain claims can be made. Certainly, there are many similarities between Huarte and Bacon, in addition to their basic classificatory system. Bacon shared Huarte's distrust of language, which he believes distracts attention from the contemplation of nature, together with his belief in the progress of the sciences. The same standpoints are to be found, however, in other sixteenth-century natural philosophers. Furthermore, the differences between Bacon and Huarte are perhaps as striking as the similarities. Bacon, to take but one example, was uncompromising in his attack on the Schoolmen,[48] whereas Huarte was lavish in his praise of the same.

Apart from Bacon, Iriarte points to echoes of the *Examen* in Richard Mulchaster, John Barclay, and other educationalists, and in philosophers such as Hobbes, Locke, and Hume,[49] but again Huarte's ideas interlock so closely with traditional notions that it is impossible, at least at the present stage of research, to be certain of direct influences. There can be no doubt as to the fact of Huarte's impact in England, however, or of continuing influence. On February 21, 1712, the *Spectator* carried an article on the *Examen* in which the various key aspects of Huarte's pedagogical theory were reviewed in detail.[50]

V   *Germany*

Huarte first figures in German scholarship as part of the flood of Spanish writing that entered Germany at the beginning of the seventeenth century, both from Dutch and Spanish presses. These included original works, translations, and adaptations of a wide variety of both didactic and imaginative literature. The *Examen* was translated into Latin by Joachim Caesar in 1622, and proved to be very successful. Caesar attempted to reconcile both of the Spanish editions, by synthesizing, contracting, and adding, but generally being fairly faithful.[51] Thus, Huarte's work found its

way into learned circles in Germany, and figured prominently in
pedagogical, philosophical, and psychological treatises, particularly after 1660, such as those by J. F. Buddeus (1699) and
Johann Justus von Einem (1734), not to mention such en-
cyclopedists as G. Stolle (1718).

The War of Spanish Succession (1701–14) awakened interest in
Spanish, which is shown by an increase in the number of gram-
mars of the language at this time. Spanish literature also continued to attract attention, particularly the work of Gracián and
picaresque novels such as *Lazarillo de Tormes*. Spanish influence
also operated via French, English, and Italian sources, radiating
from Leipzig, Dresden, and Hamburg.[52] Unlike in France, the
Examen seems to have flourished in the period of the Enlightenment in Germany. Gotthold Lessing, the famous critic and
dramatist, is the key figure. He developed an interest in Spain
from an early period (1749), stimulated by friends in academic
circles at Leipzig. Among those Spanish scholars who particularly
aroused Lessing's interest was Juan Huarte. Indeed, the German
scholar was so impressed by the *Examen* that he decided to
translate it. The finished product appeared in print in 1752,
arousing great interest.[53]

The appearance of the *Examen* in German naturally
stimulated further interest in Huarte. The educator and
philosopher of history, Johann Gottfried von Herder, was particularly fascinated by the Spaniard's discussion of climatological
influence; Goethe (c. 1770) noted the *Examen* in his diary of
reading; and J. C. Lavater (1775–78) saw Huarte as worth
reading, although full of crudities and bold, unprovable
hypotheses. However, by the time of the appearance of the second edition of Lessing's translation in 1785, the image of Huarte
had changed, and scholars were increasingly aware of the antiquated nature of many aspects of the *Examen*.

VI   *The Modern Period*

In the modern period, Huarte has continued to inspire insights
and attract scholars' attention in the many areas of investigation
that he covered in the *Examen*. The French scholar Guibelet was
one of the few scholars in previous ages to attempt anything like a
total appraisal of Huarte's work. His example was followed by
Dr. Guardia, whose analyses (1855; 1890) of the *Examen*,

whatever their imperfections, remained unsurpassed until Iriarte's full-scale work on Huarte in 1938.

The British pedagogical interest in Huarte has been continued by Foster Watson, better known perhaps for his work on Luis Vives. In March, 1905, Watson wrote an article in *The Gentleman's Magazine* that reviewed aspects of Huarte's work. He also dealt with Huarte in *The Encyclopedia and Dictionary of Education* (1921), which he edited.[54] Of course, modern British and American hispanists have continued to show some interest in Huarte, though largely in a partial and unsystematic manner.

In Germany, Huarte's name has often been associated with the work of Franz Joseph Gall (1758–1828), the German anatomist and physiologist. Gall is famous for his theory that cerebral functions are localized in various parts of the brain. Not surprisingly, Gall found Huarte of some interest in this context.[55] It is doubtful, however, whether the Spaniard was of much assistance regarding the other dimension of Gall's pioneering work, namely, the creation of phrenology or the practice of divining personality and intellect from skull shape. Besides Gall, German scholars in general continued to show an interest in the *Examen* throughout the nineteenth and early twentieth centuries. Of particular significance in this respect are H. W. Lawatz, G. I. Wenzel, T. Fritz, A. Klein, and even the philosopher Schopenhauer.[56]

In Spain, editions of the *Examen* appeared throughout the nineteenth century (e.g., Ildefonso Martínez y Fernández, 1846); Huarte's name continued to find a place in histories of medicine (e.g., Anastasio Chinchilla, 1845) and of philosophy (e.g., Luis Vidart, 1866); and isolated monographs were written (e.g., Jaime Salvá, 1841, and Mariano de Rementería, 1860). More detailed treatments of Huarte's work, however, were not forthcoming, doubtless as a result of the physician's ambiguous orthodoxy, which made Catholic writers feel rather ill-at-ease with his work. Their dilemma seems to be perfectly reflected in Marcelino Menéndez y Pelayo's monumental *La ciencia española*. Pelayo intended to counteract the tendency to denigrate the rich legacy of Spanish scholarship, and particularly the tendency to emphasize the effects of ecclesiastical repression during the sixteenth century. Huarte, of course, provided a notable example of such adverse effects, and, despite Pelayo's attempt to underplay the impact of the censors on his work, the physician proved to be a problem not easy to ignore. Huarte is given grudging recognition as a precursor of Descartes and Bacon, but Pelayo compares him unfavorably with other scholars, such as Suárez, Morcillo, and Pereira.[57] The reasons are obvious. Pelayo praises the Catholicism of Spanish scholarship, and is anxious to see materialism as a French aberration. He would tolerate no attempt to exalt Huarte, who, he continued to insist, was not a philosopher "of the first rank."[58] This was essentially the legacy passed on to the twentieth century, which the edition of the *Examen* by Rodrigo Sanz (1930), Salillas's excellent analysis (1905) of Huarte's influence on Cervantes, and Iriarte's impressive contribution have only partly rectified. It is to be hoped that the new edition by Esteban Torre will introduce more readers to the work. At least they now have ready access to a complete text of the *Examen*.

In conclusion, it is clear that, given his stature as a thinker and psychologist, Huarte remains a much neglected figure. Progress in Huartean scholarship certainly has been made in recent decades, particularly as regards our knowledge of Huarte's influence on literary theory and imaginative literature and also his influence outside Spain, although major studies of his impact in Italy and England have still to be made. Nevertheless, the calculated ambiguity of Huarte's own words, a necessary expedient forced upon him by the intolerant society in which he lived, has been compounded rather than dispelled by the partisan nature of much modern criticism. Given this continuing chaos, it is still possible for Huarte to be seen both as a precursor of Fascist racialism (Farinelli, 1936) and as a champion of human dignity (Chomsky, 1968).

CHAPTER 10

Conclusion

THE Renaissance was an age in which man turned his inquisitive eyes in many directions. Not only did he revolutionize our view of the cosmos—this was, after all, the age of Copernicus—but, through voyages of exploration, vastly extended our knowledge of the Earth itself. Scarcely less remarkable was his analysis of human nature. These advances were not carried out independently of one another. There prevailed a firm belief in the fundamental unity of the subject matter of the sciences, which, as a result, were more closely linked than they are today. Ideas and perspectives flowed freely between them, and, in particular, investigation of the human body proceeded on the assumption that certain correlations and parallels existed between the universe at large and man as a microcosm of it. The sizeable quantity of superstition retained in the very texture of science should not lead us to ignore the real progress made in many disciplines. This is especially true with respect to medicine. The age witnessed rapid advances in all branches of anatomy, physiology, and pathology. Medicine also came to set the methodological standards which guided the activity of scientists in other areas of investigation and speculation.

Spain played a key role in the expansion of medical studies in the Renaissance. The point needs to be emphasized for the simple reason that scholars have tended to adopt rather simplistic views of Spanish culture in the sixteenth century, portraying it as largely unaffected by the rise of the New Learning and committed to an all-pervasive Catholicism. While it is true that science and philosophy had a more limited development in Spain, at least in comparison with, say, Italy, we need to remember that throughout the Middle Ages medicine had flourished under Arabic rule, and Spain was renowned in the sixteenth century for its medical schools. Although in some respects an isolated and exceptional talent, Huarte clearly owes a considerable debt to this native tradition, and his work constitutes a lasting reminder that, despite the presence of the Inquisition, Spain produced thinkers as unorthodox and innovative as any in Europe.

Although we know little of Huarte the man and of the circumstances of his life, it is difficult not to feel attracted to the complex personality that emerges from the pages of the *Examen*. A retiring, private individual, profoundly aware of the difficulties attending the rationalist quest for truth, he was at the same time not without pride concerning his own achievement. Intellectually, Huarte was fearless and uncompromising, but also a man not lacking in humanity. Although sternly insistent, for example, that a student unsuited to a particular discipline should not be allowed to proceed with it, he touchingly requests that such a person be informed of the decision "with love and gentle words" (p. 72).

Huarte seems to have been a conventionally religious man. He protests his faith with apparent sincerity and speaks scathingly of the Protestant heretics. Yet one surmises that he was not a man of deep religious conviction. Indeed, it is possible he derived from Jewish stock, and consequently was neither emotionally nor intellectually committed to Christianity. His basic concern was to pursue the logic of his rationalist views wherever they might lead. That they led where they did may have surprised and disconcerted him as much as anyone, though his intellectual integrity prevented him from retracing his steps.

In retrospect, it is perhaps surprising that Huarte escaped from the clutches of the Inquisition so lightly, for there can be no doubting the basically heretical nature of his philosophy of man. We can only suppose that his protestations of orthodoxy were probably sufficient to cloud the already complex discussion in his work, and mislead an Inquisition which, although it sensed immediately the potentially dangerous nature of his ideas, seems to have been finally unable to encompass the grand design of his heresy. However, the author of the *Examen* certainly ran a terrible risk. In the face of such hostile criticism and opposition, refusal to recant in any substantial manner obviously jeopardized his life and well-being. But refuse he did. Though shunning martyrdom, he yet stubbornly and calculatingly surrendered as little as possible to the censor, and made clear his own bitterness and discontent. We are left to conclude that he was either a brave man or one so caught up by the impersonal quest for Truth that he was largely unaware of possible threats to his own safety. In either case, his work remains a striking tribute to the very spirit of science.

Ultimately, the *Examen's* fascination lies in the delicate balance it exhibits between two contrasting, contradictory views of man which have proved to be of continuing appeal. Psychology in the modern period has been dominated to a great extent by a behavioristic school, which aims at establishing a scientific study of man by focusing attention on stimuli operating upon him from without. The concept of "mind" is seen as a hangover from a pre-scientific age dominated by animistic visions of the universe, as indeed is the idea of free will. Human behavior is studied by extrapolation from that of animals, and is explained strictly in terms of conditioned response.[1] In recent decades this "ratomorphic" view of man has been increasingly challenged by a mentalistic school of thought which has stressed the uniqueness and complexity of human behavior. Mentalists present behaviorism as conducive to a dehumanizing philosophy of man, a philosophy they see as highly dangerous insofar as it involves a denial of basic human dignity.[2] It seems possible to characterize the *Examen* as an early essay in behaviorism, stemming from Huarte's profound dissatisfaction with speculative psychology, which he saw as barren, and his rejection of it in favor of a physiologically based approach. He justified such an approach by arguing that, since all men's souls are equal, differences in mental ability must reside ultimately in the physiological makeup of man. Such a view naturally favored a mechanistic explanation of human behavior and led to the progressive reduction of the realm of the spirit or mind.

We should be careful, however, not to present a one-sided view of Huarte's ideas. For despite his unflinching rationalism, the physician was never guilty of triviality in his view of man. Those aspects of human nature that he set out to explain rationally included such an elusive notion as human creativity. Indicative of the complexity of his philosophy is the fact that he has been associated with both Continental rationalism and British empiricism in philosophy. His error lay in the premature application of "scientific" explanation to the workings of the mind, and in the widespread use of the technique of analogical comparison, which often led him to oversimplify grossly.

Huarte's physiology is now virtually obsolete in its entirety, but many of his psychological insights and observations remain relevant. Some of the questions he posed, including the central one of the extent of man's natural as opposed to acquired ability, remain unsolved and as controversial as in Huarte's own day, though scholars now oppose "nature" to "nurture" rather than to "art." Much modern pedagogical theory and practice (cf. the British "Eleven Plus" Exam) concords with Huarte's belief that individuals vary congenitally in natural ability, and that, moreover, they perform with varying degrees of excellence or inability in different disciplines. On a more general level, even Huarte's teachings on the immortality of a soul represent an attempt to deal with one of the permanent problems of human destiny. It is unfortunate, therefore, that the profoundly unorthodox nature of his views should have long delayed the recognition he deserves.

Notes and References

Preface

1. For a consideration of the importance in the Renaissance of the literature of ideas, see A. J. Krailsheimer (ed.), *The Continental Renaissance: 1500–1600* (Harmondsworth: Penguin Books, 1971), pp. 16–17.

2. See Noam Chomsky, *Language and Mind* (New York: Harcourt, Brace & World, Inc., 1968), pp. 8–9.

3. Cf. Myron P. Gilmore, *The World of Humanism: 1453–1517* (New York: Harper, 1952), pp. 265–66.

4. M. de Iriarte, *El doctor Huarte de San Juan y su "Examen de ingenios": contribución a la historia de la psicología diferencial*, 3rd ed., rev. (Madrid: C.S.I.C., 1948).

Chapter One

1. The most detailed treatment of Huarte's life is still that by Iriarte, *El doctor Huarte de San Juan*, chapter I. Iriarte was able to build upon the work of Rodrigo Sanz; see prologue to Sanz's edition of the *Examen*, 2 vols. (Madrid: La Rafa, 1930).

2. See Sanz (ed.), *Examen*, I, IX.

3. See Henry Charles Lea, *A History of the Inquisition of Spain* (New York: MacMillan, 1922), I, 225–27.

4. For example, cf. Gregorio Marañón, "Juan de Dios Huarte: examen actual de un examen antiguo," in *Tiempo viejo y tiempo nuevo*, 9th ed. (Madrid: Editorial Espasa-Calpe, 1965), 115–54 (p. 115); and J. M. Guardia, "Philosophes espagnols," *Revue Philosophique*, XXX (1890), 249–94 (pp. 250–51).

5. See Sanz (ed.), *Examen*, I, X–XIII.

6. See Iriarte, *El doctor Huarte de San Juan*, pp. 30–31.

7. See Esteban Torre, *Ideas lingüísticas y literarias del doctor Huarte de San Juan* (Seville: Universidad de Sevilla, 1977), pp. 26–27.

8. Reproduced by Esteban Torre (ed.), *Examen de ingenios para las ciencias*, pp. 12–13.

9. See, for example, Arturo Farinelli, "Dos excéntricos: Cristóbal de

Villalón–El Dr. Juan Huarte," *Revista de filología española*, XXIV (1936), 9–103 (p. 67).

10. See Sanz (ed.), *Examen*, I, XI–XII.

11. See G. R. Elton, *Reformation Europe: 1517–1559* (London/Glasgow: Collins, 1963), pp. 105–12.

12. See Henry Kamen, *The Spanish Inquisition* (New York/London: Mentor Books, 1965), pp. 90–92.

13. Ibid., pp. 80–81.

14. I am thinking of Huarte's condemnation of the novels of chivalry, his profound fascination with the mystery of language, and the uninhibited and direct manner in which he confronted the Scriptures (cf. M. Bataillon *Erasmo y España*, trans. Antonio Alatorre, 2nd Spanish ed., rev. [Mexico: Fondo de Cultura Económica, 1966], pp. 75, 615–16, 693). For Erasmus's influence in Alcalá, see Bataillon, pp. 154–65. Américo Castro stresses the influence of Erasmianism on those who "aspired to let their reason follow untrodden paths and to practice the delight of self-analysis . . ." (See *Aspectos del vivir hispánico* [Madrid: Editorial Alianza, 1970], p. 113).

15. See Iriarte, *El doctor Huarte de San Juan*, pp. 87–88.

16. Guibelet, *Examen de l'Examen des Esprits* (Paris: Michel Soly, 1631), p. 539.

17. Ibid., p. 552.

18. Ibid., p. 542.

19. *The Spain of Fernando de Rojas: The Intellectual and Social Landscape of "La Celestina"* (Princeton: Princeton University Press, 1972), p. 27.

20. See, for example, *La realidad histórica de España*, 3rd. rev. ed. (Mexico: Editorial Porrúa 1966), p. 50. Contrast, however, *De la edad conflictiva*, 4th ed. (Madrid: Taurus, 1976), p. 169. Claudio Sánchez Albornoz claims that Castro greatly exaggerates the number of *conversos* among the major writers of the Golden Age (see *España: un enigma histórico* [Barcelona: Editora y Distribuidora Hispano-Americana, 1973], II, 267 ff.).

21. *El pensamiento de Cervantes*, rev. ed., with notes by author and Julio Rodríguez-Puértolas (Barcelona/Madrid: Editorial Noguer, 1972), pp. 56–57.

22. *De la edad conflictiva*, p. 153.

23. *El pensamiento de Cervantes*, p. 56.

24. Ibid., p. 57.

25. Cf. Gilman, *The Spain of Fernando de Rojas*, p. 485.

26. Ibid., p. 486.

27. Cf. Kamen, *The Spanish Inquisition*, p. 38.

28. Ibid., p. 37.

29. Ibid., p. 38.

30. Castro, *La realidad histórica de España*, pp. 280–81.

31. Cf. Gilman, *The Spain of Fernando de Rojas*, pp. 339, 340.
32. *La realidad histórica*, pp. 81–83.

Chapter Two

1. See J. L. Alborg, *Historia de la literatura española* (Madrid: Editorial Gredos, 1970), I 1014. Esteban Torre takes the opposite view: "To publish a book in Baeza in no way implied any difficulty regarding its circulation." (*Ideas lingüísticas y literarias* [Seville, 1977], p. 28).
2. See Iriarte, *El doctor Huarte de San Juan*, pp. 55–56.
3. Ibid., pp. 87–89.
4. Esteban Torre (ed.), *Examen*, p. 32.
5. Guardia, "Philosophes espagnols," *Revue Philosophique*, XXX (1890), 249–94 (p. 262).
6. Ibid., pp. 263, 284–85.
7. Ibid., p. 251.
8. Martínez y Fernández (ed.) *Examen de ingenios para las ciencias* (Madrid: Ramón Campuzano, 1846), pp. XXXI–XXXII.
9. Rementería, "Reflexiones de la obra de Juan de Dios Huarte, titulada *Examen de ingenios*," lecture given in the Central University (Madrid: Santiago Aguado, 1860), p. 10.
10. Sanz (ed.), *Examen*, I, XXI.
11. Ibid., p. XX.
12. Salinas Quijada, *Navarra: temas de cultura popular: Juan Huarte de San Juan* (Pamplona: A.G. San Juan, 1969), p. 22.
13. Salvá, "Observaciones sobre la obra titulada *Examen de ingenios*, por Juan Huarte, escritor de fines del siglo XVI," *Revista de Madrid*, III (1841), 266–76 (p. 268).
14. Hernández Morejón, *Historia bibliográfica de la medicina* (Madrid: La viuda de Jordan e hijos, 1843), III, 256.
15. *El doctor Huarte de San Juan*, p. 387.
16. Ibid., p. 54.
17. Ibid., p. 246.
18. Ibid., p. 91.
19. Ibid., p. 54.
20. Rey Altuna, "Juan Huarte de San Juan y su *Examen de ingenios*: valoración educativa actual," lecture given in the Biblioteca Provincial de Bilbao, Dec. 19, 1956, p. 8.
21. Marañón, "Juan de Dios Huarte: examen actual de un examen antiguo," in *Tiempo viejo y tiempo nuevo*, 9th ed., Madrid: Editorial Espasa-Calpe, 1965, pp. 115–54 (p. 119).
22. Farinelli, "Dos excéntricos: Cristóbal de Villalón–El Dr. Juan Huarte," in *Revista de filología española*, XXIV (1936), 9–103 (p. 63).
23. Ibid., p. 77.
24. Ibid., p. 84.

Chapter Three

1. See Richard H. Popkin, *The History of Scepticism: From Erasmus to Descartes*, rev. ed. (New York: Harper & Row, 1968), p. 3.

2. The unconscious is, of course, essentially a modern concept, and Huarte understandably had no clear conception of it (cf. Lancelot Law Whyte, *The Unconscious before Freud* [London: Anchor Books, 1962]), pp. 27–28.

3. As Sydney Pollard explains: "The first expression of the belief in progress emerged out of the creation of the new science, itself the product of the newly searching, uninhibited humanism of the Renaissance, but coming into its own in the greater intellectual freedom of the seventeenth century." (*The Idea of Progress: History and Society* [Harmondsworth: Penguin Books, 1971], p. 20).

4. For the most part Renaissance scientists were still to appreciate the value of controlled experimentation, and naturally lacked the sophisticated apparatus with which to carry it out. (See Marie Boas, *The Scientific Renaissance: 1450–1630* [London/Glasgow: Collins, 1970], pp. 235–37).

5. Other examples abound in the *Examen*. Consider, for instance, Huarte's comparison between images clearly imprinted in the memory, and therefore easy to recall, and characters clearly written by a scribe, and therefore easy to read (p. 142). Similarly, a king's pardons are compared to God's miraculous deeds in that both involve the overriding of "law" (p. 84).

Chapter Four

1. See Paul Oskar Kristeller, *Studies in Renaissance Thought and Letters* (Rome: Edizioni di Storia e Letteratura, 1956), p. 28.

2. Scholars have naturally experienced some difficulty in weighing the traditional against the innovatory aspects of the *Examen*. Huarte's originality has often been emphasized. Rementería, for example, comments upon "the daring nature of his ideas" ("Reflexiones," p. 5); Farinelli mentions Huarte's "staunch isolation" in intellectual matters ("Dos excéntricos," p. 55); and recent discussion by Transformational grammarians has again underlined Huarte's role as a precursor (e.g., Carlo Peregrín Otero, *Introducción a la lingüística transformacional* [Mexico: Siglo Veintiuno Editores, 1970], pp. 30,40). However, from the beginning, Huarte's debt to traditional scholarship has also been noted. Guibelet, one of his earliest opponents, was somewhat irritated by the Spaniard's claims to be the initiator of his science (*Examen de l'Examen*, prefatory material, no. pag.); J. M. Guardia, though insisting on the basic uniqueness of the *Examen*, reviews Huarte's debt to other writers in a scholarly and detailed manner (*Essai sur l'ouvrage de J. Huarte: Examen des Aptitudes Diverses*

pour les Sciences [Paris: A. Durand, 1855], pp. 249–54); and chapters III and IV of Iriarte's *El doctor Huarte* present an exhaustive coverage of Huarte's sources, both ancient and modern.

3. For good general treatments of Greek medicine, see Charles Singer. *A Short History of Science to the Nineteeth Century* (Oxford: Clarendon Press, 1941) and Benjamin Farrington, *Greek Science*, revised one-volume edition (Harmondsworth: Penguin Books, 1961). The most recent complete edition of the Hippocratic Corpus is that of E. Littré, *Oeuvres complètes d'Hippocrate*, 10 vols. (Paris: J. B. Baillière, 1839–61). An easily accessible selection is contained in *Hippocratic Writings*, ed. G. E. R. Lloyd, trans. J. Chadwick and W. N. Mann, I. M. Lonie, and E. T. Withington (Harmondsworth: Penguin Books, 1978). Some of the works of Galen are also available in translation: *On the Natural Faculties*, trans. A. J. Brock (London/New York: Heineman/Harvard University Press, 1963); and *On Anatomical Procedures*, ed. Charles Singer, publication no. 7 of the Wellcome Historical Medical Museum (London, 1959).

4. Huarte records Hippocrates' view thus: "Our rational soul remains always the same throughout our lives . . . ; whereas the body is never fixed in one state . . ." (p. 439).

5. After underlining Hippocrates' implicit acceptance of the influence of the body on the soul, Huarte notes: "From this, Galen ultimately concluded that all the customs and capacities of the soul, without exception, followed the temperament of the body which it [the soul] inhabits" (p. 440).

6. In view of Huarte's subtle distinction between the respective standpoints of Hippocrates and Galen, and his somewhat ambiguous attitude to the latter's, it is not surprising to find scholars divided in their analysis of Huarte's debts to tradition in this respect, their approach being dictated by their general views of the *Examen*. Hence, Marañón, for example, does not hesitate to see Huarte as a disciple of Galen ("Juan de Dios Huarte," pp. 127, 152), a view with which Guardia concurs (*Essai*, p. 253); whereas Iriarte protests: "Huarte has done Galen too great a favor by citing his treatise as the basis of the *Examen*. In actual fact, he owes very little to him. . . . How much more he owes to the incisive profundity of Hippocrates than to the pretentious redundancy of the man from Pergamum!" (*El doctor Huarte*, p. 151).

7. See G. E. R. Lloyd (ed.), *Hippocratic Writings*, p. 42.

8. See William Arthur Heidel, *Hippocratic Medicine: Its Spirit and Method* (New York: Columbia University Press, 1941), p. 62; and Lloyd, *Hippocratic Writings*, pp. 42–44. Ludwig Edelstein, however, maintains that religion and magic played a more significant part in Greek medicine than is widely believed (see "Greek Medicine in its Relation to Religion and Magic," in *Ancient Medicine: Selected Papers of Ludwig Edelstein*, eds. Owsei Temkin and C. Lilian Temkin, trans. C. Lilian Temkin [Baltimore: Johns Hopkins Press, 1967], pp. 205–46).

9. See Heidel, *Hippocratic Medicine*, p. 118.

10. See Lloyd, *Hippocratic Writings, pp.* 48–49.

11. See Kristeller, *Studies in Renaissance Thought and Letters*, p. 27.

12. Ibid., pp. 266–69.

13. See Ernst Cassirer, *The Individual and the Cosmos in Renaissance Philosophy*, trans. Mario Domandi (Oxford: Basil Blackwell, 1963), p. 43.

14. See Kristeller, *Studies in Renaissance Thought*, pp. 21–23.

15. Cf. Kristeller, op. cit., pp. 21–23.

16. Cf. J. A. Mazzeo, *Renaissance and Seventeenth-Century Studies* (London/New York: Columbia University Press/Routledge & Kegan Paul, 1964), pp. 3–22.

17. See Arthur O. Lovejoy, *The Great Chain of Being: A Study of the History of an Idea* (New York: Harvard University Press, 1957), pp. 85–86.

18. For a discussion of Scholasticism, see F. C. Copleston, *A History of Medieval Philosophy* (London: Methuen, 1972), pp. 176–229.

19. See Copleston, *A History of Medieval Philosophy*, pp. 230–33.

20. See, for example, Iriarte, *El doctor Huarte*, p. 402.

21. See Kristeller, *Studies in Renaissance Thought*, p. 561.

22. See Kristeller, "Changing Views on the Intellectual History of the Renaissance since Jacob Burckhardt" in Tensley Helton (ed.) *The Renaissance: A Reconsideration in the Theories and Interpretation of the Age* (Madison: University of Wisconsin Press, 1961), 27–52 (p. 31).

23. ". . . neither do they themselves [the followers of Aristotle] know what they mean, nor is there any man who can understand them" (p. 139). Cf. Jerrold E. Seigel, *Rhetoric and Philosophy in Renaissance Humanism: The Union of Eloquence and Wisdom: Petrarch to Valla* (Princeton: Princeton University Press, 1968), pp. 164–66, and Cesare Vasoli, *La dialettica e la retorica dell'Umanesimo* (Milan: Feltrinelli, 1968), pp. 60–61.

24. Kristeller, *Studies in Renaissance Thought*, p. 264.

25. See Kristeller, *Renaissance Concepts of Man and Other Essays* (New York/London: Harper & Row, 1972), pp. 3–6.

Chapter Five

1. See Lovejoy, *The Great Chain of Being*, particularly chapters II and III.

2. Ibid., pp. 50–59.

3. See Popkin, *The History of Scepticism*, particularly chapter III.

4. See, for example, Chomsky, *Language and Mind*, p. 9.

5. See Etienne Henry Gilson, *The Philosophy of St. Thomas Aquinas*, trans. Edward Bullough, ed. Rev. G. A. Elrington (Cambridge: W. Heffer, 1924), pp. 189–207.

6. See Cassirer, *The Individual and the Cosmos*, pp. 43–45, and *passim*.

Chapter Six

1. See Gilson, *The Philosophy of St. Thomas Aquinas*, pp. 8–32.
2. See Copleston, *A History of Medieval Philosophy*, pp. 231–32.
3. Kristeller, *Renaissance Concepts of Man*, pp. 47–48.
4. See W. P. D. Wightman, *Science in a Renaissance Society* (London: Hutchinson, 1972), p. 143.
5. Kristeller, *Renaissance Concepts of Man*, p. 28.
6. Ibid., pp. 30–31.

Chapter Seven

1. See J. R. Hale, *Renaissance Europe: 1480–1520* (London: Collins, 1971), pp. 283–97. See also Eugenio Garin, *L'Educazione umanistica in Italia: testi scelti e illustrati*, 2nd ed. enlarged (Bari: G. Laterza, 1953); and William Harrison Woodward, *Vittorino da Feltre and Other Humanist Educators*, with a foreword by E. F. Rice, Jr., (New York: Teachers College, Columbia University, 1963).
2. See R. H. Robins, *A Short History of Linguistics* (London: Longmans, 1967), pp. 17–19.
3. See R. A. Hall, Jr., "Linguistic Theory in the Italian Renaissance," *Language* 12 (1936), 96–107 (p. 98).
4. See M. K. Read and J. Trethewey, "Renaissance Ideas on the Origin and Development of Language," *Semasia* 5 (1978), 99–115 (p. 111).
5. For a discussion of Sánchez's views, see Constantino García, *Contribución a la historia de los conceptos gramaticales: la aportación del Brocense* (Madrid: C.S.I.C., 1960), p. 44. Torre has placed Huarte in perspective with respect to Sánchez (see *Ideas lingüísticas*, pp. 78–79).
6. Hall, "Linguistic Theory in the Italian Renaissance," p. 98.
7. See, for example, Chomsky, *Language and Mind*, pp. 8–9.
8. See, for example, Rey Altuna, "Juan Huarte de San Juan y su *Examen de ingenios*: valoración educativa actual" (1956).

Chapter Eight

1. As Esteban Torre writes: "Needless to say, by following his fifth instruction, not only will no male children be born—as Huarte postulates—, but, probably, no children at all." (Esteban Torre [ed.]*Examen*, p. 334, note 43.)
2. As Carlos G. Noreña writes: "The reader ought to beware of scorning the doctrine of this [final] chapter [of the *Examen*] too easily on account of its obsolete idiom and models; he should rather be encouraged to

translate Huarte's thought into the contemporary paradigm of genes and chromosomes. Only thus will he be able to appreciate the daring, originality, and incredible foresight of Huarte's thought." ("Juan Huarte's Naturalistic Philosophy of Man," in *Studies in Spanish Renaissance Thought* [The Hague: Martinus Nijhoff, 1975] [210–63 (pp. 250–51)]).

3. Cf. A. Koestler, *The Act of Creation* (London: Hutchinson, 1964), p. 224 and ff.

Chapter Nine

1. Guardiola, *Tratado de nobleza, y de los Titulos y Ditados que oy dia tienen los varones claros y grandes de España* (Madrid: La viuda de Alonso Gómez, 1595).

2. Moreno de Vargas, *Discursos de la nobleza de España* (Madrid/Paris: N. J. B. de Poilly, 1621).

3. Velázquez, *Libro de la melancolía* (Seville: H. Díaz, a costa de A. de Mata, 1585), fol. 33^r.

4. Ibid., fols. 42^v, 70^v.

5. Iriarte, *El doctor Huarte*, pp. 276–77.

6. See Martínez y Fernández (ed.), *Examen*, pp. IX–X.

7. Rodríguez, *Discernimiento filosófico de ingenios para artes y ciencias* (Madrid: Benito Cano, 1795), p. 29.

8. Ibid, pp. 30, 32, 78–83.

9. Pinciano, *Philosophia antigua poetica* (1596), ed. Alfredo Carballo Picazo, 3 vols. (Madrid: C.S.I.C., 1953), I, 37, 64, and *passim*. See also Sanford Shepard, *El Pinciano y las teorías literarias del siglo de oro*, 2nd ed. (Madrid: Editorial Gredos, 1970), pp. 28–40.

10. Carvallo, *Cisne de Apolo* (1602), ed. A. Porqueras, 2 vols. (Madrid: C.S.I.C., 1958), I, 48–49, 69–70, 70–71.

11. Ibid., I, 99–101; 11, 194.

12. Bell, *Baltasar Gracián* (Oxford: Oxford University Press, 1921), p. 56.

13. Hutchings, "The *Examen de ingenios* and the Doctrine of Original Genius," *Hispania* XIX (1936), 273–82 (pp. 280–83).

14. Ibid., p. 281 (cf. Huarte, p. 428).

15. Gracián, *Agudeza y arte de ingenio*, 3rd ed. (Buenos Aires: Editorial Espasa-Calpe, 1945), p. 17.

16. Miguel de Cervantes Saavedra, *El ingenioso hidalgo don Quijote de la Mancha*, ed. Martín de Riquer (Barcelona: Editorial Juventud, 1958), p. 19.

17. Ibid.

18. Salillas, *Un gran inspirador de Cervantes: el doctor Juan Huarte y su "Examen de ingenios"* (Madrid: Eduardo Arias, 1905), pp. 40–59.

19. Ibid., p. 115.

20. See Gerald Brenan, *The Literature of the Spanish People: From Roman Times to the Present Day* (Harmondsworth: Penguin Books, 1963), p. 171.

21. *Don Quijote de la Mancha*, e.g., pp. 123–24, 169–170, 254–55, 426, 540–41.

22. See Castro, *El pensamiento de Cervantes*, pp. 83–84.

23. Ibid., pp. 54–57.

24. Ibid, p. 351.

25. Possevino, *Cultura ingeniorum* (Venice: Io. Baptistam Ciottum, 1604), p. 24 ff.

26. Ibid., pp. 37–41.

27. Zara, *Anatomia ingeniorum et scientiarum* (Venice: A. Dei & fratrum, 1615), pp. 34, 47.

28. See Giovanni Setti, "Tassoni e Montaigne" in *Miscellanea Tassoniana di studi storici e letterari*, eds. T. Casini and V. Santi, preface by G. Pascoli (Bologna/Modena: A. F. Formiggini, 1908), pp. 227–42; and F. Nunziante, *El Conte Alessandro Tassoni ed il seicento*, preface by Duca di Maddoloni (Milan: E. Quadrio, 1885), pp. 79–83.

29. Tassoni, *Dieci libri di pensieri diversi*, aug. ed. (Venice: Marc' Antonio Brogillo, 1627), p. 249.

30. Ibid., pp. 212, 522.

31. Imperial, *Museum historicum et physicum* (Venice: Apud Juntas, 1640), p. 22.

32. See Gabriel A. Pérouse, *L'Examen des Esprits du Docteur Juan Huarte de San Juan: sa diffusion et son influence en France aux XVIe et XVIIesiècles* (Paris: Société d'Édition "Les Belles Lettres," 1976), pp. 64–69.

33. Ibid., p. 69.

34. Ibid., pp. 75–79.

35. Guibelet, *Examen de l'Examen des Esprits* (Paris: Michel Soly, 1631), p. 5.

36. Ibid., p. 16–28.

37. Ibid., p. 409.

38. Ibid., p. 386.

39. See Perouse, pp. 120–21, 140.

40. Ibid., p. 144.

41. Descartes, *Discourse on Method and the Meditations,* trans. E. E. Sutcliffe (Harmondsworth: Penguin Books, 1968), p. 39.

42. Ibid., p. 79.

43. See B. Russell, *History of Western Philosophy*, new edition (London: George Allen & Unwin, 1961), p. 551.

44. See Perouse, p. 163.

45. Ibid., p. 164.

46. See Guardia, *Essai*, p. 276.

47. See Iriarte, p. 358.

48. *The Advancement of Learning*, by G. W. Kitchin, introd. Arthur Johnson (London: J. M. Dent, 1973), p. 26.

49. *El doctor Huarte*, pp. 358, 360-2.

50. Ibid., p. 363.

51. See M. Franzbach, *Lessing Huarte-Übersetzung 1752* (Hamburg: Iberoamerikanisches Forschungsinstitut, 1965), p. 33 ff.

52. Ibid., p. 58 ff.

53. Ibid., pp. 62 ff.

54. See Iriarte, p. 364.

55. See Salvá, "*Examen de ingenios*, por Juan Huarte, escritor de fines del siglo XVI," pp. 269-76.

56. See Franzbach, chapters VI, VII.

57. *La ciencia española*, 3rd ed., 2 vols. (Madrid: Victoriano Suárez, 1933), I, 103, 105.

58. Ibid., p. 105, 116.

Chapter Ten

1. Cf. Skinner, *Beyond Freedom and Dignity* (London: Cape, 1972), pp. 17-9, and *passim*.

22. Cf. A. Koestler, *The Ghost in the Machine* (London: Hutchinson, 1967), pp. 15-18, and *passim*.

Selected Bibliography

PRIMARY SOURCES

Examen de ingenios para las sciencias. Donde se muestra la differencia de habilidades que ay en los hombres, y el genero de letras que a cada uno responde en particular. Baeza: Juan Baptista de Montoya, 1575. The early text of the *Examen*. Later editions: Pamplona (1578), Bilbao (1580), Valencia (1580), Huesca (1581), Leyden (1591 and 1652), Antwerp (1593 and 1603), Amsterdam (1662), Brussels (1702).

Examen de ingenios para las sciencias, en el qual el lector hallará la manera de su ingenio para escoger la sciencia en que más a de aprouechar. Y la differencia de habilidades que ay en los hombres, y el genero de letras y artes que a cada uno responde en particular. Baeza: Juan Baptista de Montoya, 1594. The revised text. Later editions: Medina del Campo (1603), Barcelona (1607), Alcalá (1640), Madrid (1668), Granda (1768).

Examen de ingenios para las ciencias. Edited by Ildefonso Martínez y Fernández. Madrid: Ramón Campuzano, 1846. First of the modern editions of Huarte's work. The editor's prologue still rewards a reading.

———. Edited by Adolfo de Castro. Madrid: Biblioteca de Autores Españoles, vol. LXV, 1873. Reprinted in 1905, 1913, 1929, and 1953. For all its inadequacies, this edition has had the merit of often being the only one readily available to the average reader.

———. Edited by Rodrigo Sanz. 2 vols. Madrid: Biblioteca de Filósofos Españoles, La Rafa, 1930. An outstanding comparative edition of the 1575 and 1594 versions of the *Examen*. Sanz's prologue is particularly valuable for the fresh material it provides regarding Huarte's life.

———. Edited by Emiliano Aguado. Madrid: Meléndez Valdés, 1944. An interesting selection of passages from Huarte's work. In the prologue, Aguado attempts to interpret Huarte as a social reformer and utopian dreamer.

———. Edited by Esteban Torre. Madrid: Editora Nacional, 1976. Contains an excellent introduction and up-to-date bibliography. The details of the suppressions, corrections, and additions are given in full.

TRANSLATIONS

French

*Anacrise, ou parfait jugement et examen des esprits propres et naiz aux
sciences.* Translated by Gabriel Chappuys. Lyon: Estinne Brignol,
1580.

L'examen des esprits pour les sciences. Translated by Charles Vion Dalibray. Paris: Jean le Bouc, 1645.

L'examen des esprits pour les sciences. Translated by François Savinien
d'Alquié. Amsterdam: Jean de Ravenstein, 1672.

Italian

Essame de gl'ingegni de gli huomini per apprender le scienze. Translated
by Camillo Camilli. Venice: Aldo, 1582.

*Essamina de gl'ingegni de gli huomini accommodati ad apprender qual
si volgia scienza.* Translated by Salustio Gratii. Venice: Barezzo
Barezzi, 1600.

English

Examen de Ingenios. The Examination of Men's Wits. Translated by
Richard Carew. London: Adam Islip, 1594. A modern facsimile edition is available from the Da Capo Press, Amsterdam/New York,
1969.

Examen de Ingenios, or the Tryal of Wits. Translated by Edward Bel-
lamy. London: Gray-Inn-Gate for Richard Sare, 1698.

Latin

Scrutinium ingeniorum pro iis qui excellere cupiunt. Translated by Aes-
chacius Maior (Ioachimus Caesar). Leipzig: In Officina Cothoniensi,
1622.

Dutch

Onderzoek der byzondere Vernuftens Eygentlijkke Abelheen. Translated
by Henryk Takama. Amsterdam: Johannes van Ravensteyn, 1659.

German

Johann Huarts Prüfung der Köpfe zu den Wissenschaften. Translated by
Gotthold Ephraim Lessing. Zerbst: Zimmermann, 1752.

SECONDARY SOURCES

ALBORG, JUAN LUIS. *Historia de la literatura española.* 2nd revised edition. 2 vols. Madrid: Editorial Gredos, 1970. Provides a short but
good, readily available summary of Huarte's basic philosophy.

BATAILLON, MARCEL. *Erasmo y España: estudios sobre la historia
espiritual del siglo XVI.* Translated by Antonio Alatorre. 2nd revised Spanish edition. Mexico: Fondo de Cultura Económica, 1966.
Does not deal with Huarte, but invaluable for an understanding of
the background to the age.

CASTRO, AMÉRICO. *De la edad conflictiva*. Madrid: Taurus, 1976. Contains only fleeting references to Huarte, but, like Bataillon's work, is vital for an understanding of the physician's times.

――――. *El pensamiento de Cervantes*. Revised edition by Julio Rodríguez-Puértolas. Barcelona: Noguer, 1972. Certain traits of Huarte's thought are seen as typically *converso*.

CHOMSKY, NOAM. *Language and Mind*. New York: Harcourt, Brace & World, Inc., 1968. Huarte is seen as a forerunner of seventeenth-century scholars who claimed that language and creative thought are uniquely human capacities.

FARINELLI, ARTURO. "Dos excéntricos: Cristóbal de Villalón–el Dr. Juan Huarte." *Revista de filología española*, XXIV (1936), 9–103. Well researched but highly personal in its approach. Farinelli was understandably apprehensive (given the time when he was writing) about the "racist" overtones he glimpsed in Huarte's concern with the individual's inalienable nature.

FRANZBACH, MARTIN. *Lessings Huarte-Übersetzung, 1752: Die Rezeption und Wirkungsgeschichte des "Examen de ingenios para las ciencias," 1575, in Deutschland*. Hamburg: De Gruyter, 1965. The standard work on Huarte's impact in Germany.

GILMAN, STEPHAN. *The Spain of Fernando de Rojas: The Intellectual and Social Landscape of "La Celestina."* Princeton: Princeton University Press, 1972. Essential for a full understanding of the problems faced by the *converso* in Inquisitorial Spain.

GREEN, OTIS HOWARD. *Spain and the Western Tradition: The Castilian Mind in Literature from El Cid to Calderón*. 4 vols. Madison/Milwaukee: University of Wisconsin Press, 1963–. Especially informative regarding Huarte's views on free will.

――――. *The Literary Mind of Medieval and Renaissance Spain: Essays by Otis H. Green*. Introduction by John E. Keller. Lexington: University of Kentucky Press, 1970. Contains two essays on Huarte's influence on Cervantes.

GUARDIA, JOSE MIGUEL MAGIN. *Essai sur l'ouvrage de J. Huarte: Examen des Aptitudes Diverses pour les Sciences*. Paris: A. Durand, 1855.

――――. "Philosophes Espagnols: J. Huarte." *Revue Philosophique*, XXX (1890), pp. 249–94. Two detailed studies of all aspects of Huarte's life and work. Clear, incisive, and of lasting value.

GUIBELET, JOURDAIN. *Examen de l'Examen des Esprits*. Paris: Michel Soly, 1631. A not very accessible text, but rigorously argued in its attack upon the *Examen*.

HUTCHINGS, C. M. "The *Examen de ingenios* and the Doctrine of Original Genius." *Hispania*, XIX (1936), 273–82. An attempt to trace Huarte's impact upon the Sevillian school of poetry of the late sixteenth century and upon Gracián.

IRIARTE, MAURICIO DE. *El doctor Huarte de San Juan y su "Examen de in-*

genios": contribución a la historia de la psicología diferencial. 3rd revised edition. Madrid: Consejo Superior de Investigación Científica, 1948. The standard work on the *Examen.*

KAMEN, HENRY. *The Spanish Inquisition.* New York/Toronto: Mentor Books, 1965. Does not deal directly with the author of the *Examen,* but provides an excellent treatment of the impact of the Inquisition upon the intellectual life of Spain.

MARAÑÓN, GREGORIO. "Juan de Dios Huarte: examen actual de un examen antiguo" in *Tiempo viejo y tiempo nuevo,* 9th edition. Madrid: Editorial Espasa-Calpe, 1965 (pp. 115–154). An influential essay which, when it first appeared in *Cruz y Raya,* Nov. 1933, pp. 72–120, did much to counterbalance the neglect of the *Examen* in Spain.

MENÉNDEZ Y PELAYO, MARCELINO. *La ciencia española.* 3rd edition. 2 vols. Edited by Miguel Artigas. Madrid: Victoriano Suárez, 1933. Contains brief, generally unfavorable references to Huarte, whose unorthodoxy made him somewhat uncongenial to such a profoundly Catholic scholar as Menéndez y Pelayo.

NOREÑA, CARLOS G. "Huarte's Naturalistic Philosophy of Man" in *Studies in Spanish Renaissance Thought.* The Hague: Martinus Nijhoff, 1975 (pp. 210–63). A good, well-balanced discussion, particularly valuable for its comments on Huarte's eugenics.

PÉROUSE, GABRIEL A. *L'examen des esprits du docteur Juan Huarte de San Juan: sa diffusion et son influence en France aux XVIᵉ et XVIIᵉ siècles.* Paris: Les Belles Lettres, 1970. The standard work on Huarte's influence in France.

READ, MALCOLM K. "A Re-appraisal of Juan Huarte's Concept of Creativity." *Revista española de lingüística,* año 5, Fasc. 2, Julio-Diciembre (1975), 423–32. Argues against the claim that Huarte associated language with man's creative capacity.

REMENTERÍA, MARIANO DE. *Reflexiones de la obra de Juan de Dios Huarte, titulada Examen de ingenios: discurso leído ante el claustro de la universidad central.* Madrid: Santiago Aguado, 1860. Summarizes the central theses of the *Examen.*

REY ALTUNA, LUIS. *Juan Huarte de San Juan y su "Examen de ingenios": valoración educativa actual (conferencia pronunciada en la sala de la Biblioteca Provincial de Bilbao, el día 19 de diciembre de 1956).* La Junta de Cultura de Vizcaya. A discussion of Huarte's relevance to modern pedagogical theory and practice.

SALILLAS, RAFAEL. *Un gran inspirador de Cervantes. El doctor Juan Huarte y su "Examen de ingenios."* Madrid: Eduardo Arias, 1905. The pioneering study of Huarte's impact on Cervantes.

SALINAS QUIJADA, FRANCISCO. *Navarra: temas de cultura popular.* Pamplona: A. G. San Juan, 1969. Contains a detailed account of Huarte's life with a brief appraisal of the significance of his work.

SALVÁ. JAIME. "Observaciones sobre la obra titulada *Examen de ingenios por Juan Huarte, escritor a fines del siglo XVI*" in *Revista de Madrid*. 3rd series (1841), 266–76. Largely a comparison of Huarte's ideas with those of the German phrenologist Gall.

TORRE. ESTEBAN. *Ideas lingüísticas y literarias del doctor Huarte de San Juan*. Publicaciones de la Universidad de Sevilla, 1977. A detailed study of Huarte's ideas on language viewed in the context of his times. Chomsky's interpretation of Huarte is found wanting.

Index

Abril, Pedro Simón, 58
Adam, 70, 92
Advancement of learning, The (Bacon), 121
Adversa fortuna de Don Bernardo Cabrera, La (Lope de Vega), 112
Albornoz, Claudio Sánchez, 130n20
Alcalá, The University of, 15, 17, 19, 85, 130n14
Álvarez, Diego, 28, 106
Animadversión y enmienda de algunas cosas que se deben corregir en el libro que se intitula "Examen de ingenios" (Álvarez), 28
Antoniana Margarita (Pereira), 118
Aquinas, St. Thomas, 48, 56, 65–66, 72, 75, 92
Aristotelianism, 15, 33, 54–55, 56, 79, 80
Aristotle, 37, 41, 43, 44, 48, 53, 54–55, 56, 61, 62, 63, 64, 65, 78, 79–81, 82, 83, 90–92, 93, 97, 116
astrology, 66, 103
Augustine, St., 48, 53, 55–56, 71, 78
Ávila, Juan de, 24

Bacon, Francis, 121, 124
Barclay, John, 121
Bayle, Pierre, 120
Bell, A.F.G., 108
Bellay, Edward, 120
Bodin, Jean, 117
Boscán Almugáver, Juan, 107
Bouchet, Guillaume, 117
Bruno, Giordano, 47, 77
Buddeus, J.F., 122

Caesar, Joachim, 121
Camilli, Camillo, 114, 120
Carew, Richard, 120

Carvallo, Luis, 108
Castro, Américo, 20, 21, 23, 113, 130n14, 130n20
Cervantes, 110–114, 115, 124
Chanet, Pierre, 118
Chappuys, Gabriel, 116, 117, 119
Charles V, 14, 18, 21, 22
Charron, Pierre, 117, 118
Chinchilla, Anastasio, 123
Chomsky, Noam, 124
Christ, 22, 23, 70, 76
Cicero, 48, 64, 88, 92
Ciencia española, La (Menéndez y Pelayo), 123
Cisneros. *See* Ximénez de Cisneros
Colonna, Cardinal Ascanio, 115
conceptismo, 108–109
conversos, 19–24, 112, 130n20
Copernicus, 77, 125
Counter-Reformation, The, 18, 114
Cratylus (Plato), 53
creativity, 26, 30, 54, 55–56, 60, 62–67, 70, 87, 107, 108
Cusanus, Nicholas, 54

D'Albret, Jean, 14
De Doctrina Christiana (St. Augustine), 55
Democritus, 111
Descartes, 118–119, 124
determinism, 27, 31, 32, 33, 60, 70, 108, 113, 114, 119, 120
Dictionnaire Historique et Critique (Bayle), 120
Don Quijote (Cervantes), 110, 112
Duns Scotus, John, 56, 79, 92

Einem, Johann Justus von, 122
Enlightenment, The, 107, 120, 122
Erasmus, 18, 19, 112, 130n14

145

Essays (Montaigne), 115, 116–117
Examen de l'Examen (Guibelet), 118

Farinelli, Arturo, 33, 124, 132n2
    (Chapter Four)
Feijóo, 107
Ferdinand the Catholic, 14
Ficino, Marsiglio, 54
Fortune, 77–78, 97
Francis I, 22
free will, 33, 70, 83, 114
Fritz, T., 123

Galatea (Cervantes), 110
Galen, 16, 48–49, 51, 61, 68, 69,
    74, 76, 81, 82–83, 106, 115, 133n5,
    133n6
Galileo, 55
Gall, Franz Joseph, 123
Gentleman's Magazine, The (Watson),
    123
Gilman, Stephen, 20
Goethe, 122
Gracián, Baltasar, 108–109, 122
Grajal, Gaspar de, 19
Granada, Fray Luis de, 19
Gratii, Salustio, 114
Guardia, J.M., 31–32, 33, 122, 132n2
    (Chapter Four), 133n6
Guardiola, Benito, 106
Guibelet, Jourdain, 20, 118, 122,
    132n2 (Chapter Four)

Hall, Jr., R.A., 93
Herder, Johann Gottfried von, 122
Hernández Morejón, Antonio, 32
hidalguía, 24, 66–67, 97, 106
Hippocrates, 48–49, 51–53, 83, 93,
    111, 133n5, 133n6
Hobbes, 121
Humanism, 17, 18, 45, 56, 57–58, 75,
    85–88
Hume, 121
Hutchings, C.M., 108

Imperial, Juan, 116
Inquisition, The, 14, 16, 17, 18–20,
    28–31, 32–33, 61, 73, 75, 126
In Praise of Folly (Erasmus), 112
insanity, 26, 69, 110–113

Iriarte, M. de, 32, 121, 123, 124,
    133n2, 133n6

Jews, 19–24, 68, 126
Judaism. *See* Jews

Kamen, Henry, 21
Klein, A., 123
Kristeller, Paul Oskar, 57, 73, 78

Laguna, Dr. Andrés de, 21
Lavatar, J.C., 122
Lawatz, H.W., 123
Lazarillo de Tormes, 122
León, Fray Luis de, 19, 24
Le Pailleur, 120
Lerma, Pedro de, 19
Lessing, Gotthold, 122
Licenciado Vidriera, El (Cervantes),
    112
Locke, 121
López Pinciano, Alonso, 108
Luther, 18, 19, 35, 71

Marañón, Gregorio, 33, 133n6
Martínez de Cantalapiedra, Martín,
    19
Martínez y Fernández, Ildefonso, 31,
    32, 123
materialism, 31, 119, 124
Menéndez y Pelayo, Marcelino, 123
Mersenne, Marin, 118
Montaigne, 47, 115, 116–117
Montesquieu, 120
Morcillo, Sebastián Fox, 124
Moreno de Vargas, Bernabé, 106
Mulchaster, Richard, 121

Nebrija, Antonio de, 15, 17
Neoplatonism, 60, 78

Ockam, William of, 56, 72
Otero, Carlos Peregrín, 132n2
    (Chapter Four)

Paracelsus, 47
Pascal, 120
Pascual, Mateo, 19
Pensieri diversi (Tassoni), 115
Pereira, Gómez, 31, 58, 118, 124

Petrarch, 55
Philip II, 16, 19, 29, 86, 89, 96
Pico della Mirandola, Giovanni, 54
Plato, 48, 53–54, 60, 61, 62, 63,
    65, 74, 75, 76, 78, 81, 83, 90–92,
    93, 107–108, 118
Platonism, 53–54, 78
Pomponazzi, Pietro, 55, 73, 79
Pope Pius IV, 92
Possevino, Antonio, 114–115, 116
Pretel, Dr. Alonso, 28
Prometheus, 66

Quijada, Francisco Salinas, 32
Quintilian, 48

Rementería, Mariano de, 32, 123,
    132n2 (Chapter Four)
Rey Altuna, Luis, 33
Rodríguez, Ignacio, 107
Rojas, Fernando de, 21, 24
Romanticism, 107

Sagesse (Charron), 117, 118
Salillas, Rafael, 110, 124
Salvá, Jaime, 32, 123
Sánchez el Brocense, Francisco, 19, 90
Sánchez the Skeptic, Francisco, 21, 24
    40
Sanz, Rodrigo, 32, 124
Scholasticism, 33, 45, 54, 56, 57, 66,
    78, 92–94, 121
Schopenhauer, 123
Silhon, Jean, 118
skepticism, 35–46, 61, 75, 79, 113,
    119

Socrates, 43, 53
Stolle, G., 122
Suárez, Francisco, 124

tabula rasa, 56, 62, 63, 65
Tassoni, Alessandro, 115–116
Teresa St., de Ávila, 24
Torre, Esteban, 124, 131n1, 135n1
    (Chapter Eight)
*Treatise of the Education and Learn-
    ing Proper for the Different
    Capacities of Youth, A* (Bellay), 120
Triall of Wits, A (Wolf), 120

Valdés, Juan de, 19
Valla, Lorenzo, 57
Valles, Francisco, 15
Vega, Cristóbal de, 15
Vega, Lope de, 112
Velasco, Águeda de, 15
Velázquez, Andrés, 106
Versalius, 49
Vidart, Luis, 123
Villalobos, Dr. Francisco, 21
Villavicencio, Lorenzo de, 28
Vion Dalibray, Charles, 118, 119–120
Vives, Luis, 21, 24, 58, 121, 123

Watson, Foster, 123
Wenzel, G.I., 123
Wolf, John, 120

Ximénez de Cisneros, Cardinal
    Francisco, 17, 18

Zara, Antonio, 115, 116